Debbie Mumm's New Expressions

Dear Friends,

I am so fortunate to get to do what I do. Even after 20 years, and 50 books, the passion is still here and the ideas (thankfully) keep on coming. As I planned our celebration for my 20th anniversary in business, I decided that the two books that I would do during my anniversary year should have special significance. The first, called *Memories and Milestones* is a collection of quilts to celebrate life's many milestones mixed with my own memories of my first 20 years in business. For this, my second 20th anniversary year book, I wanted to look forward and focus more on trends, colors, and some contemporary styles of decorating with fabric. I'm very pleased and excited about the result, which is aptly titled, *New Expressions*.

We really had fun experimenting with new techniques, developing color stories for each chapter, using a variety of fabrications, and looking at different ways to enhance a home with easy fabric, painting, and craft projects. Blending traditional quilting with contemporary colors and decorating styles gave us the opportunity to stretch our wings and reveal some fresh ways to express our creativity with fabric and paint. I hope that this book will also inspire you to stretch a little, try new techniques, experiment with colors, and take your love of quilting and fabric crafting to a new level.

With this book, we launch the next twenty years of creativity. I hope that you will join us on this journey of expression and joy. Keep doing what you love!

My best,

Debbie Mumm

table of con

Contemporary

Introduction 4

Contempo Twin Quilt 6

Simple Sham 8

Digital Daze Pillow 10

Day Bed Bolsters 11

Go With The Flow
    Pillow 12

Peaceful Pillow 13

Illusion Throw 14

Floral Expressions
    Triptych 18

Renewal

Introduction 22

Sun and Shadow
    Wall Quilt 24

Sun and Shadow
    Table Runner 26

Leaf Printed Pillows 28

Rock & Twig Table 30

Garden Bench Update . . 32

Stone Birdhouse 33

Rock and Rope
    Flowerpot 33

Reflection

Introduction 34

Radiance Table Runner . .36

Color-Banded
    Chandelier 38

Finishing Touches
    Napkins and
    Napkin Rings 38

Reflected Glory
    Votive Holder 39

Flamboyant Flowers
    Wall Art 40

Rhythm

Introduction 44

Rhythm & Blues
    Bed Quilt 46

Upbeat Tempo
    Wall Art 50

Easy Display Shelves 52

Displaying Collections . . .53

Buttons Squared Pillow . . 54

Dotted Dashes Pillow 55

Easy Pillow Shams 55

tents

Imagination

Introduction. 56

Diamondback Chair 58

Imagination Desk. 62

Bits n Pieces Boxes 63

Treasure Box 64

Daisy Wall Quilt 66

Sophistication

Introduction. 68

Elegance Squared
Throw 70

Multi Metal Lamp 72

Square on Square
Wall Art. 74

Curlicue Wall Art 76

Horizon Wall Art 77

Expression

Introduction. 78

Contemporary Expression
Wall Art 80

Geometric Pillow 82

Seminole Style Quilt 84

Update with Paint 88

Serenity Pillow 90

Box Pillows 91

Et Cetera

About This Book. 2

General Directions 92

About Debbie 96

Credits. 96

"Creativity involves
breaking out of
established patterns in
order to look at things
in a different way."

--Edward De Bono

Contemporary

Sleek modern lines,

clean design in fashion-conscious

colors, abstract details,

pared-down accessories,

and color-blended wall art

create a comfortable

and modern living space.

Contempo Twin Quilt

Oversized blocks and strip-piecing make this quilt fast and easy, yet the color combination and overall quilting make this quilt contemporary and compelling. Used on a day bed or in a bedroom, this quilt will set the scene for fun and fashionable living. Dressed-up with monochromatic shams and a medley of unique pillows, this quilt is simply sensational.

Contempo Twin Quilt 71" x 103"	FIRST CUT	
	Number of Strips or Pieces	Dimensions
Fabric A Light Green Stripe 2¾ yards	12 12	4¼ " x 42" 3½ " x 42"
Fabric B Medium Brown Stripe ¾ yard	12	2" x 42"
Fabric C Tan Stripe 1½ yards	12 12	2½ " x 42" 1½ " x 42"
Fabric D Dark Green Stripe 1½ yards	12	4¼ " x 42"
Fabric E Dark Brown Stripe ⅝ yard	12	1½ " x 42"
BORDERS		
First Border ½ yard	9	1½ " x 42"
Outside Border ¾ yard	9	2½ " x 42"
Binding ¾ yard	9	2¾ " x 42"
Backing - 6½ yards Batting - 79" x 111"		

Fabric Requirements & Cutting Instructions

Read all instructions before beginning and use ¼ "-wide seam allowances throughout. Read Cutting Strips and Pieces on page 92 prior to cutting fabrics.

Getting Started

Twenty-four blocks are arranged in two different positions to add movement and interest to the quilt. The large 16½" (unfinished) strip-pieced blocks are easily made. Two borders and binding finish the quilt. Use a combination of see-through rulers to mark 16½" squares on the strip-pieced sections.

Refer to Accurate Seam Allowance on page 92. Whenever possible, use the Assembly Line Method on page 92. Press seams in direction of arrows.

Making the Quilt

1. Arrange and sew one 4¼" x 42" Fabric A strip, one 2" x 42" Fabric B strip, one 1½" x 42" Fabric C strip, one 4¼" x 42" Fabric D strip, one 1½" x 42" Fabric E strip, one 3½" x 42" Fabric A strip, and one 2½" x 42" Fabric C strip together as shown. Press. Make twelve.

Tip—When sewing several strips together, turn the unit after each strip is added to alternate the direction of sewing from one row to the next.

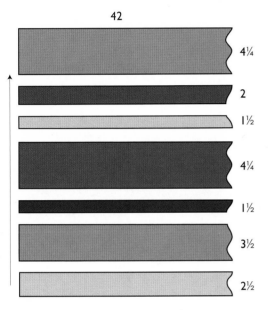

42

4¼

2

1½

4¼

1½

3½

2½

Make 12

2. Cut twenty-four 16½" squares from strip sets as shown. See Tip Box at right for ways to measure a large block. Leftover strip set pieces can be used for Digital Daze Pillow on page 10.

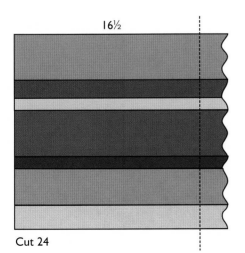

16½

Cut 24

3. Referring to photo and layout, arrange and sew four blocks together to make a row. Make six rows. Press seams in opposite directions from row to row.

4. Arrange and sew rows together. Press.

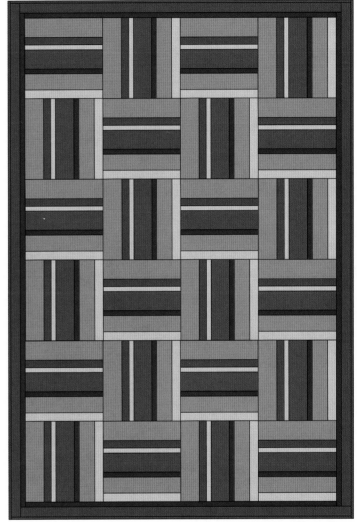

Contempo Twin Quilt
Finished Size: 71" x 103"

Tip— There are several ways to measure a block that may be larger than a ruler.

a. Place two or more rulers together side-by-side to equal the measurement needed. Align straight edges of ruler with seam lines to ensure a square block.

b. Make a template using paper or poster board being careful to ensure lines are parallel and perpendicular.

c. Use a gridded cutting mat aligning edges of strip-pieced unit to ensure block is square.

Adding the Borders

1. Sew 1½" x 42" First Border strips together end-to-end to make one continuous 1½"-wide border strip. Press. Measure quilt through center from side to side. Cut two 1½"-wide First Border strips to this measurement. Sew to top and bottom of quilt. Press seams toward border.

2. Measure quilt through center from top to bottom including borders just added. Cut two 1½"-wide First Border strips to this measurement. Sew to sides of quilt. Press.

3. Refer to steps 1 and 2 to join, measure, trim, and sew 2½"-wide Outside Border strips to top, bottom, and sides of quilt. Press.

Layering and Finishing

1. Cut backing crosswise into two equal pieces. Sew pieces together to make one 80" x 117" (approximate) backing piece. Press.

2. Arrange and baste backing, batting, and top together referring to Layering the Quilt on page 94.

3. Machine or hand quilt as desired.

4. Sew 2¾"-wide binding strips end-to-end to make one continuous 2¾"-wide binding strip. Refer to Binding the Quilt on page 94 and bind quilt to finish.

simple sham

Finished Size: 18½" x 27"

Soft tonal neutrals and a geometric design make these shams a soothing backdrop for the vibrant Contempo Twin Quilt.

Getting Started

This sham is quick and easy to piece. It is not quilted, but can be with the addition of 23" x 31" pieces of batting and lining and following the instructions in step 1, Finishing Pillows on page 95. Use ¼"-wide seam allowances throughout. Our instructions are for one sham.

Simple Sham 18½" x 27" Material for One Sham	FIRST CUT		SECOND CUT	
	Number of Strips or Pieces	Dimensions	Number of Pieces	Dimensions
Fabric A Center and Borders ½ yard	1	15½" x 42"	1	15½" x 6½"
			2	3¾" x 21½"
			2	3½" x 19"
Fabric B First Border ¼ yard	2	3½" x 42"	2	3½" x 15½"
			2	3½" x 12½"
Backing ¾ yard	2	12" x 42"	2	12" x 27½"
Standard Pillow Hook and Loop tape (Optional)				

Making the Sham

1. Sew 15½" x 6½" Fabric A piece between two 3½" x 15½" Fabric B pieces as shown. Press.

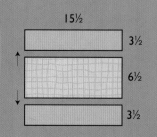

15½

3½

6½

3½

2. Sew unit from step 1 between two 3½" x 12½" Fabric B pieces as shown. Press.

3½   3½

12½

3. Sew unit from step 2 between two 3¾" x 21½" Fabric A pieces as shown. Press.

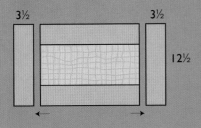

21½

3¾

3¾

4. Sew unit from step 3 between two 3½" x 19" pieces as shown. Press.

3½   3½

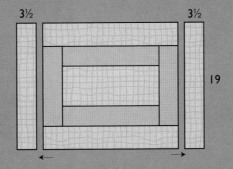

19

5. Make a narrow hem on backing pieces. Fold one 27½" edge of backing fabric under ¼" to wrong side. Press. Fold under ¼" again to wrong side and press. Stitch along folded edge. Make two.

6. With right sides up, lay one backing piece over second piece so hemmed edges overlap and backing measures 19" x 27½". Baste backing pieces together at sides where they overlap as shown.

27½

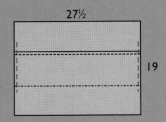

19

7. With right sides together, position and pin sham top to backing. Using ¼"-wide seam, sew all edges together. Remove basting. Trim corners, turn right side out, and press. Insert one standard bed pillow. If a tighter fit is desired, sew hook and loop tape to overlapped edges on backing.

Pillows and more Pillows

Nothing dresses a bed, sofa, or day bed like pillows! Choose from a variety of sizes, styles, and ornamentation to make pillows that perfectly express your personal taste.

This dynamic pillow can either be made from left-over pieces from the Contempo Twin Quilt or easily constructed with the strip-piecing method.

Materials Needed

Pillow Center – End pieces from Contempo Twin Quilt Strip Sets
OR
Fabric A - ⅛ yard Light Green
    One 4¼" x 16"
    One 3½" x 16"
Fabric B - ⅛ yard Med. Brown
    One 2" x 16"
Fabric C - ⅛ yard Tan
    One 2½" x 16"
    One 1½" x 16"
Fabric D - ⅛ yard Dark Green
    One 4¼" x 16"
Fabric E - ⅛ yard Dark Brown
    One 1½" x 16"
Pillow Border and Backing - ⅝ yard
    Two 16½" x 13" pieces for backing
    Two 16½" x 3½" pieces
    Two 14½" x 3½" pieces
Pillow Form Fabric - ⅔ yard
    Two 20½" x 16½" pieces
Polyester Fiberfill
Five Green Buttons

Digital Daze Pillow

Finished size: 16" x 20"

Getting Started

Leftover strip-pieced sections from Contempo Twin Quilt, page 7, step 2 can be used to make the center of this pillow. Skip to step 2 if these pieces are available.

Making the Pillow

1. Arrange and sew the following pieces as shown:
    4¼" x 16" Fabric A
    2" x 16" Fabric B
    1½" x 16" Fabric C
    4¼" x 16" Fabric D
    1½" x 16" Fabric E
    3½" x 16" Fabric A
    2½" x 16" Fabric C
    Press.

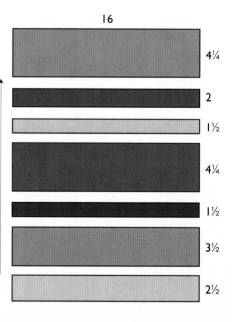

2. Using unit from step 1 OR Contempo Twin Quilt leftover strip set units, cut three 2½"-wide segments and four 1½"-wide segments as shown.

2½ 2½ 2½ 1½ 1½ 1½ 1½

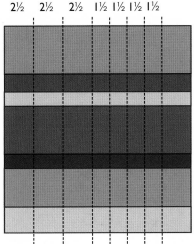

3. Alternating and off-setting units by ½" sew units together as shown. Press.

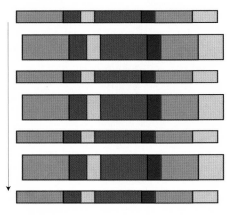

4. Using a see-through ruler and rotary cutter, trim sides of unit from step 3 to make a 14½" x 10½" rectangle as shown.

14½

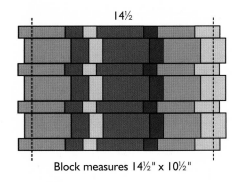

Block measures 14½" x 10½"

5. Sew unit from step 4 between two 14½" x 3½" Border pieces. Press. Sew this unit between two 16½" x 3½" Border pieces as shown. Press. Embellish pillow with buttons.

6. Refer to Finishing Pillows, page 95, steps 2-4, and use two 16½" x 13" backing pieces to sew backing.

3½   14½   3½

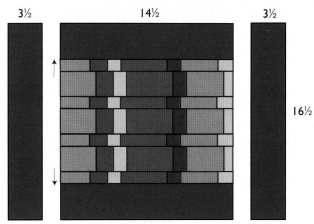

16½

7. Referring to Pillow Forms, page 95, use two 20½" x 16½" Pillow Form pieces and fiberfill to make 20" x 16" pillow form.

Day Bed Bolsters

Finished size: 26" x 6"

Materials Needed for One Bolster

Fabric - ⅝ yard
    One 21" x 30" piece
    One 6½" circle
Cord - ¾ yard
Two 6" x 14" Bolster Forms

Making the Bolster

1. With right sides together, fold 21" x 30" fabric piece in half lengthwise and sew a ½"-wide seam leaving a ½" opening ¾" from one edge as shown.

Press seam open. This opening will make a slot for the cord.

30   ⌐Fold⌐

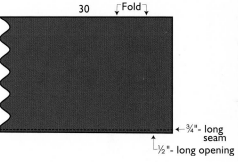

←¾"- long seam
½"- long opening

2. On edge with opening, fold raw edge of fabric ¼" to wrong side and press. Fold again ½" and press to form a hem. Edge stitch hem to make an enclosure for the cord.

3. With right sides together, pin 6½" fabric circle to remaining end of unit from step 2 easing curved edges. Sew pieces together using a ¼"-wide seam allowance. Press.

4. Turn bolster cover right side out. Insert cord into cord enclosure.

5. Insert two bolster forms in bolster cover. Holding both ends of cord, pull cord to gather end of bolster. Tie cord and tuck inside opening.

Go with the Flow Pillow

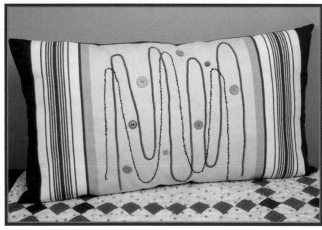

Finished size: 28" x 15"

Materials Needed

Fabric A (Pillow Center) - ½ yard
    One 14½" x 15½" piece
Fabric B (Striped Border) - ¼ yard
    Two 5½" X 15½" pieces
Fabric C (Outside Border & Backing) - ⅝ yard
    One 15½" x 25½" piece (backing)
    One 15½" x 10½" piece (backing)
    Two 2½" x 15½" pieces
Two Decorative Yarns - 2¼ yards of each
Assorted Buttons
Temporary Adhesive Spray
Pillow Form Fabric - ⅞ yard
    Two 28½" x 15½" pieces
Polyester Fiberfill

Getting Started

An easily pieced pillow top makes the backdrop for free form yarn design and buttons. The backing has an opening close to the side so a pillow form can be easily inserted.

Making the Pillow

1. Arrange and sew two 2½" x 15½" Fabric C pieces, two 5½" x 15½" Fabric B pieces, and 14½" x 15½" Fabric A piece together as shown at right. Press.

2. Place pillow top right side up on a flat surface. Spray center of pillow (Fabric A) with temporary adhesive spray. Referring to photo, arrange yarns and buttons on fabric. Apply gentle pressure to yarn to lightly secure in place. Mark positions of buttons.

3. Refer to Couching Technique on page 95 and couch yarns. Arrange and sew on buttons.

4. Make a narrow hem on backing pieces. Fold one 15½" edge of 15½" x 25½" backing fabric under ¼" to wrong side. Press. Fold under ¼" again to wrong side and press. Stitch along folded edge. Repeat with one 15½" edge of 15½" x 10½" backing piece.

5. With right sides up, lay one backing piece over second piece so hemmed edges overlap and backing measures 28½" x 15½". Baste backing pieces together as shown.

28½

15½

6. With right sides together, position and pin pillow top to backing. Using ¼"-wide seam, sew around edges. Trim corners, turn, and press.

7. Refer to Pillow Forms on page 95 and use two 28½" x 15½" pieces of fabric to make pillow form. Insert pillow form.

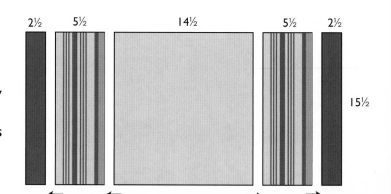

2½   5½   14½   5½   2½

15½

Finished size: 16" square

Materials Needed

Fabric A (Pillow & Backing Center) - ¼ yard
　　One 5½" x 16½" piece
　　Two 5½" x 11" pieces (backing)
Fabric B (Pillow & Backing Sides) - ½ yard
　　Two 6" x 16½" pieces
　　Four 6" x 11" pieces (backing)
Leaf Appliqué Fabric - Scraps
Lightweight Fusible Web - ⅛ yard
Lining - 20" square
Batting - 20" square
16" Pillow Form

Getting Started

Bright green and bold brown make a striking backdrop for the quick-fused leaves. The backing mimics the pillow top so the pillow is attractive at any angle.

Making the Pillow

1. Sew 5½" x 16½" Fabric A piece between two 6" x 16½" Fabric B pieces as shown. Press.

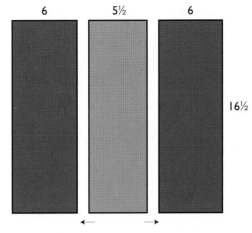

2. Refer to appliqué instructions on page 93. Our instructions are for Quick-Fuse Appliqué, but if you prefer hand appliqué, add ¼" seam allowances. On paper side of fusible web, trace nine leaves.

3. Use Leaf Appliqué Fabric to prepare appliqués for fusing.

4. Referring to photo, position and fuse nine leaves to pillow top. Finish edges with satin stitch or other decorative machine stitching as desired.

5. Refer to Finishing Pillows, page 95 step 1, to prepare pillow top for quilting. Quilt as desired

6. Sew one 5½" x 11" Fabric A piece between two 6" x 11" Fabric B pieces as shown. Press. Make two.

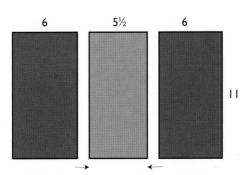

Make 2

7. Make a narrow hem on backing pieces. Fold one 16½" edge of unit from step 6 under ¼" to wrong side and press. Fold under ¼" again to wrong side and press. Stitch along folded edge. Make two.

8. With right sides up, lay one backing piece from step 7 over second backing piece so hemmed edges overlap and unit measures 16½" square. Baste backing pieces together as shown.

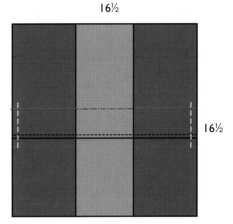

9. With right sides together, position and pin pillow top to backing. Using ¼"-wide seam, sew around edges. Trim corners, turn, and press. Insert 16" pillow form.

Leaf
Make 9

Illusion Throw

Illusion Throw 41" x 59"	FIRST CUT		SECOND CUT	
	Number of Strips or Pieces	Dimensions	Number of Pieces	Dimensions
Fabric A Green Background ⅞ yard	3	9½" x 42"	9	9½" squares
Fabric B Gold Background ⅝ yard	2	9½" x 42"	8	9½" squares
Fabric C Tan Background ⅝ yard	2	9½" x 42"	7	9½" squares
BORDERS				
Border ½ yard	5	2½" x 42"		
Binding ½ yard	5	2¾" x 42"		

Backing - 2⅝ yards
Batting - 47" x 65"
Gold Appliqués - ⅓ yard
Dark Green Appliqués - ⅓ yard
Orange Appliqués - ⅓ yard
Brown Appliqués - ⅙ yard
Lightweight Fusible Web (17" wide) - 3 yards
Template Plastic
Stabilizer

Fabric Requirements & Cutting Instructions

Read all instructions before beginning and use ¼"-wide seam allowances throughout. Read Cutting Strips and Pieces on page 92 prior to cutting fabrics.

Getting Started

Bright colored blocks look complicated, but are easy and fast to make for this throw. Blocks are 9½" square unfinished and arranged in a random order.

Refer to Accurate Seam Allowance on page 92. Whenever possible, use the Assembly Line Method on page 92. Press seams in direction of arrows.

Echo Quilting and diamond appliqués create a secondary motif within this impressive quilt. The simple elliptical appliqués create the illusion of movement and the subtle color combination evokes a feeling of nature. It's amazing that a quilt that's so simple to construct can create so many moods!

Making the Quilt

Refer to appliqué instructions on page 93. Our instructions are for Quick-Fuse Appliqué, but if you prefer hand appliqué, add ¼" seam allowances. We recommend using stabilizer for machine appliqué.

1. Refer to Quick-Fuse Appliqué on page 93 and Ellipse Pattern on page 16. Use template plastic to make a template of pattern. Press fusible web to wrong sides of 12" x 36" pieces of gold, dark green, and orange appliqué fabrics.

2. On paper side of fusible web, trace thirty-six elliptical shapes for gold fabric, thirty-two shapes for dark green fabric, and twenty-eight shapes for orange fabric. Cut out shapes.

3. Fold one 9½" Fabric A square in half then in fourths to mark center of square. Referring to pattern layout on page 16, position and fuse four gold elliptical shapes to right side of one 9½" Fabric A square as shown, making sure appliqués are inside seam allowances. Make nine. Finish appliqué edges with machine satin stitch or other decorative stitching as desired.

Make 9

4. Referring to step 3, position and fuse four dark green eliptical shapes to one 9½" Fabric B square. Make eight. Position and fuse four orange elliptical shapes to one 9½" Fabric C square. Make seven. Finish appliqué edges with machine satin stitch or other decorative stitching as desired.

Make 8   Make 7

5. Arrange and sew four assorted blocks to make a row as shown. Press. Referring to photo on page 14 and layout on page 16, make six rows. Press seams in opposite directions from row to row.

Make 6 in assorted combinations

6. Press fusible web to wrong side of 6" x 20" brown appliqué fabric piece. With a rotary cutter and see through ruler, cut eighteen 2" squares.

7. Fold one row from step 5 in half lengthwise to mark center of row. Position and fuse three 2" brown appliqués to row as shown in center of each block seam. Finish appliqué edges with machine satin stitch or other decorative stitching as desired. Make six.

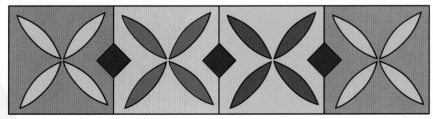

Make 6 in assorted combinations

8. Referring to photo and layout on page 16, sew rows together. Press.

Adding the Borders

1. Measure quilt through center from side to side. Cut two 2½"-wide border strips to this measurement. Sew to top and bottom of quilt. Press seams toward border.

2. Sew 2½" x 42" border strips together end-to-end to make one continuous 2½"-wide border strip. Press. Measure quilt through center from top to bottom including borders just added. Cut two 2½"-wide border strips to this measurement. Sew to sides of quilt. Press.

Layering and Finishing

1. Cut backing crosswise into two equal pieces. Sew pieces together to make one 47" x 80"(approximate) backing piece. Press and trim to 47" x 65".

2. Arrange and baste backing, batting, and top together referring to Layering the Quilt on page 94.

3. Machine or hand quilt as desired.

4. Sew 2¾"-wide binding strips end-to-end to make one continuous 2¾"-wide binding strip. Refer to Binding the Quilt on page 94 and bind quilt to finish.

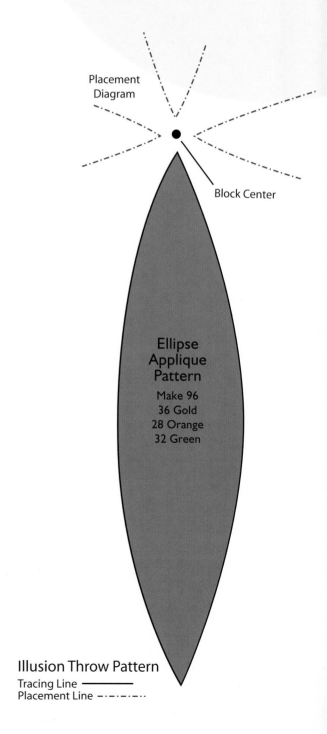

Placement Diagram

Block Center

Ellipse Applique Pattern
Make 96
36 Gold
28 Orange
32 Green

Illusion Throw Pattern
Tracing Line ———
Placement Line ─·─·─·─

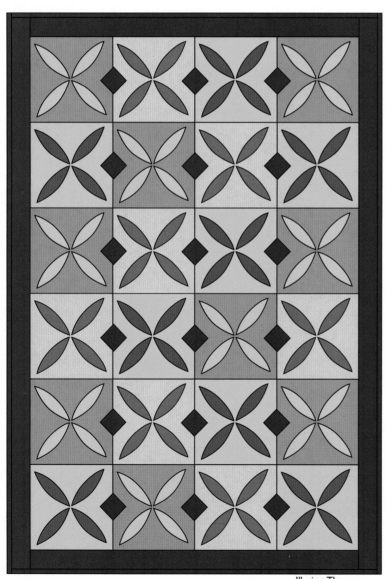

Illusion Throw
Finished Size: 41" x 59"

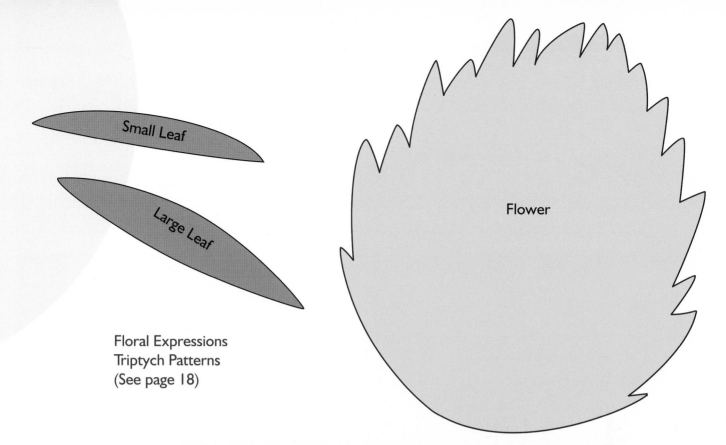

Small Leaf

Large Leaf

Flower

Floral Expressions
Triptych Patterns
(See page 18)

Square Vase

Floral Expressions Triptych

Each Panel measures 11½" x 30"

Express your artistic nature and experiment with new techniques to create your own wall art to match a quilt or your home décor. The easy techniques and new products used to create this complementary wall trio will give you inspiration and ideas for wall pieces to use throughout your home. Because of drying time of dimensional paint, allow several days to complete this project.

Supply List

¾" Thick MDF Board (available at hardware stores) - Three 11½" x 30" pieces

Liquitex® Acrylic Gesso

Delta Texture Magic Dimensional Paint™ - Two tubes, light color

Clear Stencil Material such as .005 mm Acetate (clear report covers from an office supply store work well and are inexpensive) - Four 8½" x 11" sheets

Craft Knife

Masking Tape

Palette Knife

Assorted Paintbrushes

Burnt Umber Water Based Glaze Effects*

Pencil, Ruler, Fork

Cording for Stems

Liquitex® Tube Acrylic Paints -
    Orange Background:
        Burnt Sienna
        Red Oxide
    Orange/Gold Highlights:
        Vivid Red Orange
        Cadmium Yellow Medium
    Brown Background:
        Burnt Amber
        Raw Sienna
    Vases and Leaves:
        Chromium Oxide Green
        Brilliant Yellow Green

Decoupage Medium

Three Hangers

*This environment friendly glaze is available at American Unfinished Furniture Stores. If unavailable, mix a few drops of burnt umber acrylic paint with water-based clear glaze for a substitute.

Note: Because we wanted heavy textures, acrylic paints in tubes were used instead of the craft paints in bottles that we commonly use. If desired, bottle paints can be substituted for tube paints.

Making the Wall Art

1. Refer to General Painting Directions on page 95. Using a wide paintbrush, apply a coat of Gesso to the MDF Boards. When thoroughly dry, sand at an angle with coarse sandpaper. Repeat process two or three times sanding in a different direction each time. This creates texture on painting surface.

2. Tube acrylics were used for this project because they are much thicker and give the project more texture. Two colors are used for the burnt orange background (see supply list). Apply the colors simultaneously but without mixing them together so the background has a mottled effect. Apply paint to all three boards at the same time so colors match. Brush paint on in various stroke directions for more texture. Allow to dry.

3. Add orange/gold highlights to the background as shown.

4. Line up all three boards on a table. Referring to photo, use a pencil to mark lines for placement of brown color on each board. Use two shades of brown and repeat step 2 to add brown color to background.

5. Using patterns on pages 17 and 21, trace three vase patterns, flower, and both leaves on individual pieces of stenciling material. Place stenciling material on a surface suitable for cutting, and using a craft knife, cut out each stencil as shown. Mark top side of each stencil with a piece of tape to avoid confusion later.

6. Using photo on page 18 as a placement guide, plan the placement of each element on prepared boards. Draw a pencil line where stems will be.

7. Use masking tape to temporarily hold a vase stencil to each board. Make sure bottom of each vase is parallel to bottom of board. On our boards, Square Vase is 3¾" from bottom, Zigzag Vase is 2¼" from bottom, and Triangular Vase is 3" from bottom.

8. Using dimensional paint and a palette knife, spread dimensional paint over one vase stencil as shown.

9. Use palette knife, fork, or pencil to add details to vase while dimensional paint is still wet. Repeat for other two vases.

10. Carefully pull back stencil while paint is still wet and clean stencil for a later use.

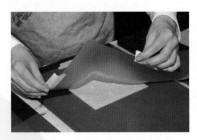

11. Repeat process for each vase, then add flower heads and middle row of leaves. Make sure that stencil material doesn't overlap any wet areas. You may need to trim away some of the stencil material to avoid overlapping. Be very careful not to smudge wet paint. Allow to dry overnight.

12. Repeat steps 9, 10, and 11 to add remaining leaves to each board. Make sure that stencil material doesn't overlap any wet areas. Allow to dry overnight before painting.

13. Replace the cleaned stencils over each of the vases and use masking tape to secure. The stencils will mask off the background areas making it much easier to paint each element.

14. Apply a basecoat of medium green paint to each vase. Dry brush lighter green paint as shown for added color and texture.

15. Using stencils to mask the background, paint flowers and leaves using the same technique and colors noted on supply list.

16. Lay pieces of cording for stems on a flat surface. Apply brown paint to the cording and allow to dry.

17. Use decoupage or a glue that dries clear to attach stem cording to painted boards. Allow to dry thoroughly.

18. Apply burnt umber glaze to each art piece, applying more glaze where deeper color is desired and removing glaze with a damp cloth where less color is desired. The glaze will blend the colors and add a soft sheen to the entire art piece. It will also gather in depressions so that the details in the vases will stand out.

19. When dry, attach a hanger to the back of each board, protecting the painted surface by setting the board on a towel.

Floral Expressions
Triptych Patterns

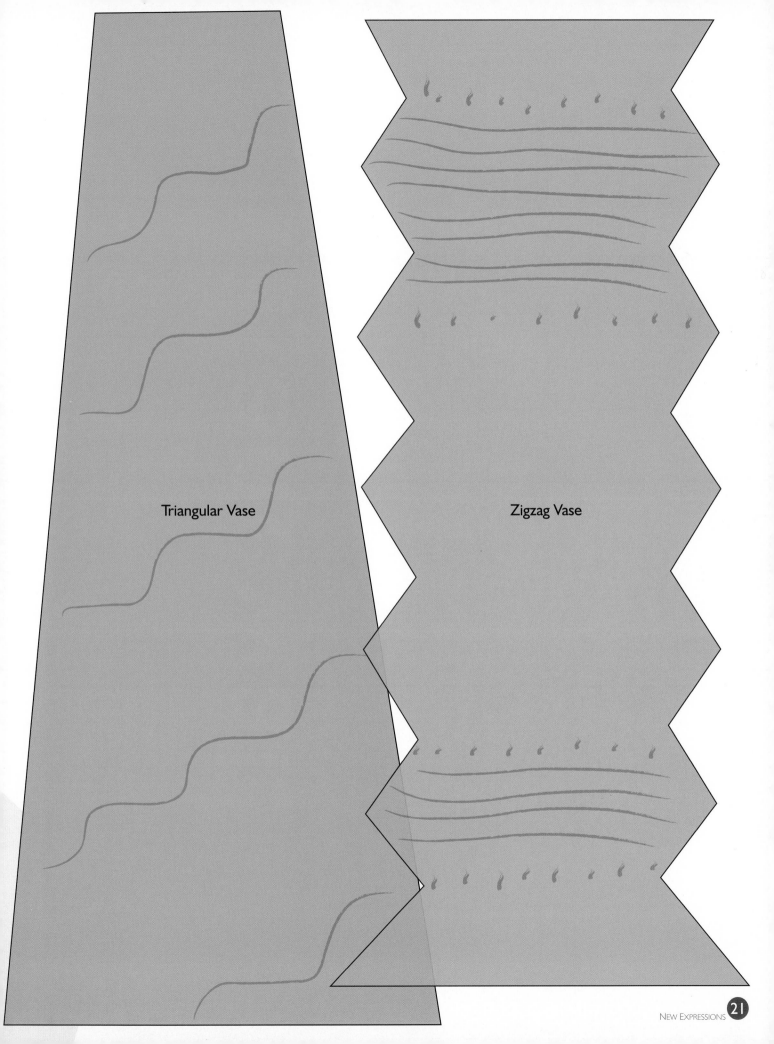

Triangular Vase

Zigzag Vase

Renewal

That which is old becomes new again to create a natural setting for relaxation. The spirit, too, is renewed with a wall quilt showcasing nature's colors. Harmonious, yet random leaf shapes are sponge printed on a trio of porch pillows.

Sun and Shadow Wall Quilt

A play of soft and strong colors creates a sunshine and shadows pattern on this easy-to-live-with wall quilt. Use fabrics from your stash to create strip sets which are then cut on the diagonal to form the blocks. Diagonal cuts create a sewing challenge, which is easily handled with our sewing tips.

Sun and Shadow Wall Quilt 41" x 29"	FIRST CUT		SECOND CUT	
	Number of Strips or Pieces	Dimensions	Number of Pieces	Dimensions
Fabric A Light Strips ⅛ yard each of ten fabrics	2*	1⅝" x 42" *Cut for each fabric	4*	1⅝" x 21"
Fabric B Medium value strips ⅛ yard each of five fabrics	2*	1⅝" x 42" *Cut for each fabric	4*	1⅝" x 21"
Fabric C Dark Strips ⅛ yard each of five fabrics	2*	1⅝" x 42" *Cut for each fabric	4*	1⅝" x 21"
BORDERS				
Border ⅓ yard	4	2½" x 42"		
Binding ⅜ yard	4	2¾" x 42"		
Backing - 1¼ yards Batting - 45" x 33" Template Plastic				

Fabric Requirements and Cutting Instructions

Read all instructions before beginning and use ¼"-wide seam allowances throughout. Read Cutting Strips and Pieces on page 92 prior to cutting fabrics.

Getting Started

Strip-pieced units cut into triangles and joined together make shaded units, 6½" square unfinished. Assorted fabrics alternated from unit to unit give the appearance of a scrap quilt. Two strips each of twenty different fabrics make the strip-pieced units. Use an assortment of ten light fabrics, five medium value fabrics, and five dark fabrics to make ten light strip sets and ten medium/dark strip sets. Since the triangles are cut on the bias, the use of a walking foot is recommended for joining the blocks.

Refer to Accurate Seam Allowance on page 92. Whenever possible, use the Assembly Line Method on page 92. Press seams in direction of arrows.

Making the Blocks

1. Arrange Fabric A strips in stacks of four, alternating placement and order of fabrics.

2. Arrange Fabric B and C strips in stacks of four, alternating placement and order of fabrics.

3. Sew Fabric A strips together in sets of four as shown. Press. Make ten strip sets. Sew Fabric B and C strips in sets of four. Press. Make ten strip sets.

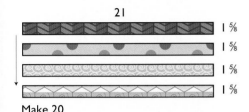

21

1 ⅝
1 ⅝
1 ⅝
1 ⅝

Make 20
(10 light sets and 10 medium/dark sets)

4. On a large piece of template plastic, draw a right angle triangle with two sides 7⅜" long as shown. Cut out template and use to mark triangles on each strip set from step 3. From each strip set, cut two or three triangles to equal twenty-four light triangles and twenty-four medium/dark triangles.

7⅜"

7⅜"

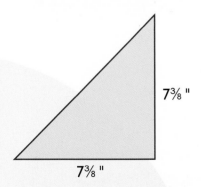

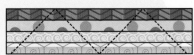

Cut 48
(24 assorted light triangles and 24 assorted medium/dark triangles)

5. Sew one light triangle to one dark triangle to make a square as shown. Press. Make twenty-four. Square to 6½".

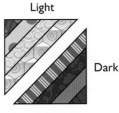

Light

Dark

Make 24
Square to 6½"

6. Referring to photo on page 24 and layout on page 26, determine layout of quilt by arranging units in four rows of six units each. **Press seams in direction of arrows for each section as shown prior to assembling 12½" blocks.**

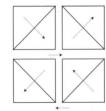

7. Using a walking foot to minimize stretching, sew two units from step 6 together as shown. Press carefully to avoid stretching. Make twelve and press seams according to diagram in step 6. If a walking foot isn't available, stay-stitch a scant ¼ inch from edges of each unit before sewing units together. This will help to maintain the shape of each unit when sewing diagonal edges together.

Make 12
May need to re-press seams

8. Sew two units from step 7 together as shown, rotating blocks so seams fall opposite each other at intersections Press. Make six. Block measures 12½" square.

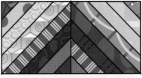

Make 6
Block measures 12½" square

9. Referring to photo on page 24 and layout on page 26, sew units from step 8 together to make quilt top. Press.

Adding the Borders

1. Refer to Adding the Borders on page 94. Measure quilt through center from side to side. Cut two 2½"-wide border strips to that measurement. Sew to top and bottom of quilt. Press seams toward border.

2. Measure quilt through center from top to bottom including borders just added. Cut two 2½"-wide border strips to that measurement. Sew to sides of quilt. Press.

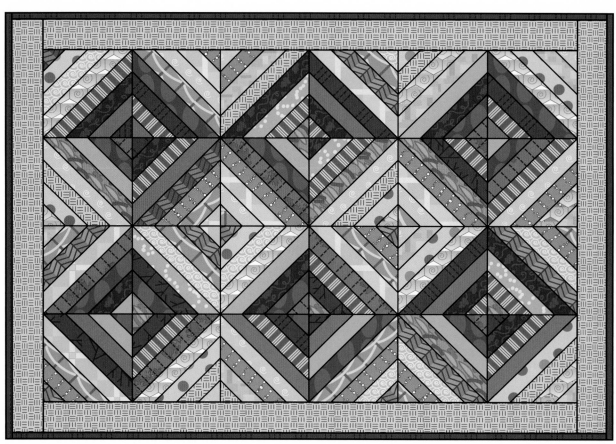

Sun and Shadow Wall Quilt
Finished size: 41" x 29"

sun and shadow table runner

Add the delightful play of soft and strong colors to your dining table by creating a table runner using the same techniques as the wall quilt.

Materials Needed:

Refer to Sun and Shadow Wall Quilt Cutting Chart on page 24.
Increase Border fabric to ½ yard, five 2½" x 42" strips.
Increase Binding to ½ yard, five 2¾" x 42" strips.

Making the Blocks

1. Make Sun and Shadow Blocks following steps 1-8 on page 25.

2. Arrange and sew blocks in a long row as shown. Press seams in one direction.

3. Sew 2½"-wide Border strips together end-to-end to make one continuous 2½"-wide Border strip. Refer to Adding the Borders, steps 1 and 2, on page 94 to add borders.

Layering and Finishing

1. Cut backing fabric to 45" x 33". Arrange and baste backing, batting, and top together referring to Layering the Quilt on page 94. Hand or machine quilt as desired.

2. Sew 2¾" binding strips end-to-end to make one continuous 2¾"-wide binding strip. Refer to Binding the Quilt on page 94 and bind quilt to finish.

Layering and Finishing

1. Cut and sew backing fabric to measure 22" x 83". Arrange and baste backing, batting, and top together referring to Layering the Quilt on page 94. Hand or machine quilt as desired.

2. Sew 2¾" binding strips end-to-end to make one continuous 2¾"-wide binding strip. Refer to Binding the Quilt on page 94 and bind table runner to finish.

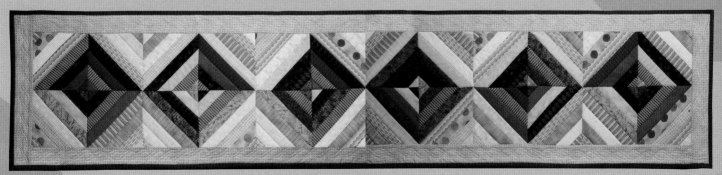

Sun and Shadow Table Runner
Finished size: 17" x 77"

Leaf Printed Pillows

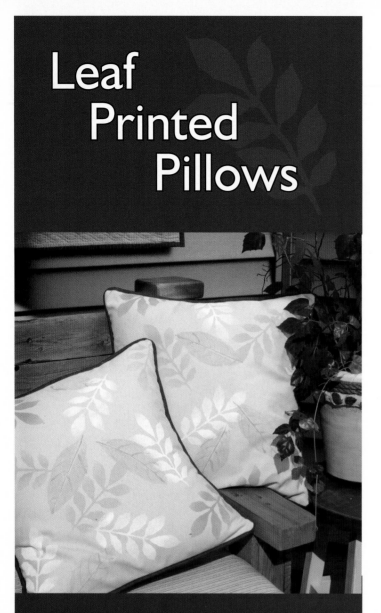

Create your own leafy fabric for these nature-loving pillows that are perfect for a porch or sun room. Two easy techniques are used to create the leaf-strewn look, and fabric medium makes the paint permanent and pliable. Experiment on fabric scraps to get comfortable with the techniques before applying to pillow fabric.

Supply List (Makes One 17" Square Pillow)

Tan Cotton Duck or Canvas Fabric - ⅞ yard
    One 18" square
    Two 12" x 18"
Brown Piping Fabric - ¼ Yard
Piping Cord - 2 Yards
18" Pillow Form
Americana® Fabric Painting Medium - 2 oz. Bottle
Americana® Acrylic Craft Paints - Light Buttermilk, Antique White, Golden Straw, Antique Gold
Delta Ceramcoat® Acylic Craft Paint - Raw Sienna
Leaf Frond Stencil - A wide variety of stencils are available at most craft stores.
Small Foam Roller
Fresh Leaf (We took ours from a house plant)
Palette Paper or Plastic Disposable Plate
Assorted Paintbrushes

Painting the Fabric

Refer to General Painting Directions on page 95.

1. Cut one 18" square from pillow fabric and place on plastic-covered work surface.

2. Using photo for inspiration, decide on general placement of leaves and colors for your pillow. Following directions on Fabric Painting Medium, mix medium with paints as they are used.

3. Place a teaspoon size pool of Light Buttermilk paint on palette paper. Roll sponge roller in paint/medium mix until well covered.

4. Place stencil on fabric, tape in several places to secure if desired, then roll color over stencil as shown to form leaf fronds. Do all Buttermilk colored fronds at one time, making sure that stencil does not overlap on any freshly applied paint. Rinse stencil and wash out roller and dry with paper towels.

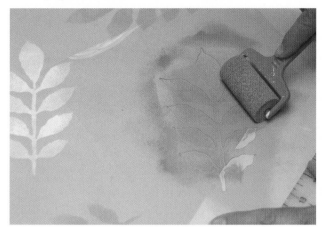

5. Repeat steps 3 and 4, with Antique White and Raw Sienna paint colors. Allow each color of paint to dry thoroughly before applying the next color.

6. A fresh leaf pulled from a house plant or tree is used as a 'stamp' for the next process. Select a leaf with deep veins in a shape that you like. Using a paint brush, carefully coat underside of leaf with Golden Straw paint, adding some Antique Gold at edges. Use a fine paint brush and Raw Sienna paint to outline the veins as shown.

7. Carefully turn leaf over and position on pillow fabric with paint side down.

8. Use firm roller to transfer paint from leaf to fabric. Carefully pull up leaf making sure not to smear paint. Repeat process to add leaves where desired on pillow fabric. Allow to dry thoroughly

Making the Pillow

Use ½"-wide seams throughout.

1. Cut brown piping fabric into 2½"- wide strips. Sew piping strips together end-to-end to make one continuous 2½" x 80" (approximate) strip.

2. Cover cording with piping strip. Using a zipper foot, baste close to cording. Pin piping to right side of printed pillow piece overlapping piping 2".

3. Refer to Box Pillows, page 91, steps 4-7, to sew piping to pillow.

4. Refer to Finishing Pillows on page 95, steps 2-4. Use two 12" x 18" fabric pieces to make backing.

Rock & Twig Table

Renew your spirit and decorate your home with the rich gifts of Nature. This small coffee table is at once functional and beautiful...even more so since it is made from found items and recycled materials! Smooth stones and rough twigs combine for textural interest and color contrast while still providing the soothing essence of natural elements to the coffee table top. An old rolling file holder was adapted for the table base.

Supply List

Scrap Lumber
Small Table (or similar to become the table base)
Delta Ceramcoat Acrylic Craft Paint® - Burnt Umber
Burnt Umber Water Based Glaze Effects*
Spray Satin Varnish
Assorted Paintbrushes
¼" Thick Plate Glass to Fit Table Top (sanded edges recommended)
Premixed Ceramic Tile Adhesive and Grout
Putty Knife or Palette Knife
Assorted Stones (Bags of stones are available at craft stores.)
Wood Glue, Nails, Screws
Straight Twigs

*This environment friendly glaze is available at American Unfinished Furniture Stores. If unavailable, mix a few drops of burnt umber acrylic paint with water-based clear glaze for a substitute.

Making the Coffee Table

Recycled lumber and an old file holder form the basis for this extraordinary coffee table. A piece of glass adds a smooth surface to the table while still allowing the rock and twig decoration to show through. Look around your garage or basement or check yard sales for a salvageable piece to use as your coffee table base. Refer to General Painting Directions on page 95.

1. To adapt the file holder to become a base for the table, we simply cut off the legs to the height desired (16" for base; overall height is 18½"). The size of your table top should be based on the scale of the base you select.

Before

2. Top portion of the coffee table is constructed like a shadow box frame. Ours measures 19" x 26" with mitered corners and is 2½" deep. Cut a ½"-thick piece of plywood to fit inside the frame and form the bottom of the table top. Glue and nail the bottom in place.

3. Cut narrow boards (⅜"-thick and 1¾"-wide) to fit inside the frame and rest on the plywood bottom. Glue and nail boards in place to hold the glass tabletop which is added later.

4. Sand all pieces to remove oils and old finishes. Remove sanding residue with a tack cloth or damp rag.

5. Paint all wood pieces with burnt umber paint. Two or more coats may be needed for good coverage. When thoroughly dry, sand edges for a distressed look.

6. Apply burnt umber glaze to all painted surfaces to darken sanded spots and to provide a soft sheen. Allow to dry.

7. Spray base and tabletop with Satin Varnish for a long-lasting finish.

8. Measure and have glass cut to fit inside frame resting on the ledge created in step 3.

9. Cut straight twigs to the inside width of table top and plan rock placement. Experiment with the Premixed Ceramic Tile Adhesive and Grout before working on your table. Spread adhesive/grout on a small board and press twigs and various sizes of rock into the adhesive/grout. Adhesive/grout may need to be deeper for larger rocks to obtain the desired look.

10. Using a putty knife or palette knife, carefully spread Premixed Ceramic Tile Adhesive and Grout on bottom board of table, being careful to not get adhesive/grout on the painted sides. Push twigs into adhesive/grout, placing them close together.

11. Next, push larger rocks into the grout forming the desired pattern. Complete the tabletop by adding smaller rocks. Make sure all pieces are adhered and there are no loose rocks. Allow to dry overnight.

12. Use screws to fasten tabletop to base and insert glass into frame.

Garden Bench Update

Relax on a comfortable porch surrounded by soothing plants and natural elements. This weathered bench was renewed with a little sanding and an easy-to-apply finish. Bright pillows and a custom bench pad complete the update of an old favorite.

Supply List

Wooden Bench
Palm Sander and Sandpaper
Matte Spray Varnish
Burnt Umber Water Based
   Glaze Effects*

*This environment friendly glaze is available at American Unfinished Furniture Stores. Or, mix a few drops of burnt umber acrylic paint with water-based clear glaze for a substitute.

1. Refer to General Painting Directions on page 95. Sand bench to remove weathered wood layer and to smooth grain. Start with medium sandpaper, then finish with fine sandpaper. Make any needed repairs or style changes. We chose to cut off the birdhouse tops on the supports and replace them with squares cut from 2" x 4" lumber. Birdhouse holes were filled with wood putty and the new square finials were screwed to the posts. Use a damp cloth or tack cloth to remove all sanding residue.

2. Following directions and precautions on can, apply Burnt Umber Glaze to bench, adding or wiping off glaze as needed until desired tone of wood is achieved. Allow to dry thoroughly.

3. Spray bench with one or more coats of varnish. Add a cushion and Leaf Printed Pillows (page 28) if desired to create a relaxing garden spot.

Before

Stone Birdhouse

Supply List

Unfinished Birdhouse
Premixed Ceramic Tile Adhesive
    and Grout
Small Rocks
Palette Knife
Twig
Delta Ceramcoat® Acrylic Paint -
    Burnt Umber and Spice Brown
Americana® Acrylic Paint -
    Avocado
Spray Matte Varnish

1. Refer to General Painting Directions on page 95. Paint birdhouse and roof with Burnt Umber paint and base with Avocado paint and allow to dry. Using Spice Brown and a dry brush technique, add highlights to birdhouse. Use Burnt Umber paint to add distressing to avocado base. When thoroughly dry, spray birdhouse with matte varnish.

2. Referring to photo, determine placement of stone accents. Apply a thick layer of tile adhesive/grout to stone areas and place small rocks into the adhesive/grout. Use adhesive/grout to attach a twig to the birdhouse to serve as a perch.

3. Allow adhesive/grout to dry thoroughly before using your birdhouse as a decoration in a covered area.

rock and rope flowerpot

Supply List

Terracotta Flowerpot
Artist's Gesso
Premixed Ceramic Tile Adhesive and Grout
Assorted Rocks
Sisal rope
Tacky Glue

Masking Tape
Americana® Acrylic Paint - Golden Straw and
    Buttermilk
Assorted Paintbrushes and Palette Knife
Burnt Umber Water Based Glaze Effects*

*This environment friendly glaze is available at American Unfinished Furniture Stores. If unavailable, mix a few drops of burnt umber acrylic paint with water-based clear glaze for a substitute.

1. Refer to General Painting Directions on page 95.

2. Apply Gesso to flowerpot, outside and inside, to prepare it for painting. Allow Gesso to dry thoroughly.

3. Paint base of flowerpot with Golden Straw, then the rim and inside with Buttermilk. It may take two or more coats for good coverage. Allow to dry completely.

4. Decide on placement of rocks and rope. Use masking tape to mask off painted areas on each side of rock area. Using a palette knife, apply a thick

coat of adhesive/grout and press rocks into adhesive/grout. Remove masking tape while grout is still wet.

5. To make the rope a darker color, we soaked it in burnt umber glaze and laid it out to dry.

6. Apply burnt umber glaze to entire flowerpot, adding glaze where more depth of color is desired and removing glaze with a damp cloth where less color is desired. Allow to dry completely.

7. Wrap rope around flowerpot and secure with tacky glue.

A toasty glow reflects throughout

when votives and side lamps illuminate.

Color block accessories grace a

gleaming table. A pleasing spice-

colored palette is the focus

of a graphic wall art design.

Simplicity, function and fashion are in

abundance in this warm, inviting room.

Reflection

Radiance Table Runner

Glowing colors radiate light and energy making these matching table runners a feast for the eyes. The easy strip-pieced runners are custom-made to the table size for a clean, up-to-date look.

Radiance Table Runner 63" x 14" Fabric for one Table Runner	FIRST CUT		SECOND CUT	
	Number of Strips or Pieces	Dimensions	Number of Pieces	Dimensions
Fabric A Orange Stripe ¼ yard	2	3½" x 42"	1	3½" x 7½"
Fabric B Gold Stripe ⅙ yard	1	3½" x 42"		
Fabric C Brown Stripe ⅙ yard	1	3½" x 42"		
Fabric D Dark Orange Stripe ⅙ yard	1	3½" x 42"		
Fabric E Light Green Stripe ⅙ yard	1	3½" x 42"		
Fabric F Medium Green Border ½ yard	4	4" x 42"		
Backing - 1 yard				

Fabric Requirements and Cutting Instructions

Read all instructions before beginning and use ¼"-wide seam allowances throughout. Read Cutting Strips and Pieces on page 92 prior to cutting fabrics.

Getting Started

Bold, strip-pieced stripes make the center of this table runner. The border adds the right finishing touch. There is no batting or quilting on this runner and strip-piecing speeds construction, so it can easily be made in less than a day. If you desire a longer table runner, increase Fabric B, C, D and E yardage to ¼ yard and make additonal strip sets.

Refer to Accurate Seam Allowance on page 92. Whenever possible, use the Assembly Line Method on page 92. Press seams in direction of arrows.

Making the Table Runner

1. Arrange and sew one 3½" x 42" strip each of Fabrics A, B, C, D & E as shown. Press.

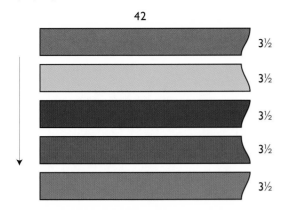

2. Cut four 7½"-wide strip-pieced sections from unit in step 1 as shown.

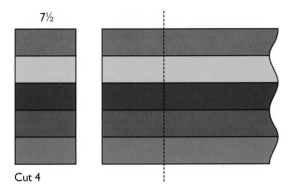

Cut 4

3. Referring to photo, arrange and sew four units from step 2 into one long piece. Sew one 3½" x 7½" Fabric A piece to end of unit as shown so unit begins and ends with orange stripe. Press. If a longer or shorter table runner is desired, add or remove 3½" x 7½" fabric pieces.

4. Sew 4" x 42" Fabric F pieces end-to-end to make one 4"-wide border piece. Measure unit from step 3 lengthwise and cut two border pieces to this measurement (Our unit measured 63½"-long). Sew unit from step 3 between two 4"-wide Fabric F pieces as shown. Press.

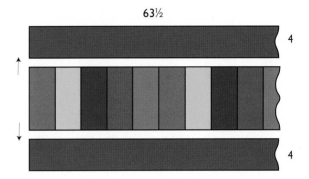

5. Cut backing fabric in half crosswise. Sew pieces together to make one 18" x 80" (approximate) backing piece. Press.

6. Arrange table runner top and backing, right sides together. Sew around edges of table runner leaving a 5" opening for turning. Trim backing even with table runner top, clip corners, turn, and press. Hand-stitch opening closed.

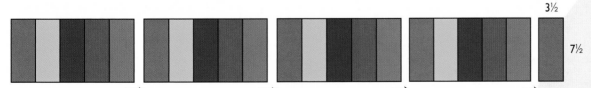

Glowing Accessories

Lighting is an important part of any room décor, and this dining room glows with both direct and reflected light. Small lamps on the buffet highlight the fabric art piece and wash the wall with a golden glow. Votive candles rest on a mirrored tray, which reflects the light and motion of the candle flames. Beaded "candlets" circle each votive adding the sheen and sparkle of beads to the eye-catching display. Overhead, a decorated shade chandelier illuminates the table with lustrous polish. With a combination of light sources, every room can glow with a warming welcome.

Color-Banded Chandelier

Illuminate your room with a ribbon-decorated chandelier that reinforces the color scheme and repeats the stripe theme.

Supply List

Drum Shade Chandelier*
Ribbons:
   Three colors ⅝"-wide ribbon -
     Amount equal to circumference
     of shade plus 2"
   Two colors 1½"-wide ribbon -
     Amount equal to circumference
     of shade plus 2"
Elmer's® Craft Bond Extra-
   Strength Spray Adhesive

*We purchased this chandelier at a major discount store. The shade is 18" in diameter and 10½" high. It came with the light fixture and cord. An alternative is to purchase a large drum shade and a lighting kit which is available at home improvement stores. For best results, shade sides should be straight up and down rather than angled.

it's in the details

Add the finishing touches to a lovely table with these reversible napkins and beaded napkin rings.

Supply List for Two Napkins

Fabric A - ½ yard
  Two 16½" squares
Fabric B - ½ yard
  Two 16½" squares

Making the Napkins

1. Position and sew 16½" Fabric A and Fabric B squares, right sides together, using a ¼"-wide seam allowance and leaving a 4" opening for turning.

Making the Shade

1. Ribbons in a variety of textures and colors are adhered to a plain shade for a dressed-up, yet contemporary, look for this dining room. This is a two person job because spray adhesive needs to be applied in segments and the ribbon applied and smoothed quickly. Be sure to practice the process with scrap ribbons and an old lamp shade (or something similar) before tackling your shade. Double stick tape was used to temporarily hold our ribbons when deciding on placement. If desired, put small pencil marks on shade to mark position of each ribbon.

2. Protect work surface with cardboard or paper and read and follow directions on spray adhesive. Starting with bottom ribbon, spray about one-fourth of length and apply to shade, smoothing ribbon carefully. Using paper to protect shade and nearby surfaces, spray the next fourth and continue in this way until first ribbon is applied. Trim off excess ribbon, allowing ribbon to overlap about ½" in the back. Follow this procedure for all ribbons. Allow to dry and hang fixture as desired.

Reflected Glory Votive Holder

Golden light from candle flames and lamps is enhanced and reflected by a simple mirror tray. Sparkly beaded bracelets encircle each votive holder for even more shine.

Supply List

Purchased Mirror with Wood Frame
Sandpaper, Masking Tape & Assorted Paintbrushes
Acrylic Craft Paint (your choice of color)
Burnt Umber Glaze*
Glass Votive Holders & Candles
Assorted Beads and Elastic Cord
Four 1" Wooden Ball Knobs
Wood Glue

*This environment friendly glaze is available at American Unfinished Furniture Stores. If unavailable, mix a few drops of burnt umber acrylic paint with water-based clear glaze as a substitute.

A purchased mirror is painted and elevated to become a tray holder for votive candles.

Use masking tape to mask off mirror. Sand frame to remove sheen and paint with acrylic craft paint. Two coats may be necessary for good coverage. Paint wooden ball knobs to match. When thoroughly dry, apply burnt umber glaze to add texture. Glue ball knobs to bottom of mirror. String beads on elastic cord to fit around each votive holder, secure with a knot. Assemble as shown in photo.

2. Clip corners and turn right side out. Press. Hand-stitch opening closed.

3. Edge-stitch or top-stitch close to edge of napkins.

Making the Napkin Rings

Because we chose a bold print for our napkins, the napkin rings feature a simple design and color scheme. A shell pendant attached to each beaded napkin ring makes a bold statement without a lot of fuss.

Supply List

Beads - Assorted colors and sizes

Elastic Cording - Two 6" pieces

Shell Pendants - Two with jump rings.

String beads on elastic cording in pattern desired and add shell pendant. Napkin rings should measure approximately 2" in diameter. Tie cording securely and put a drop of clear glue on knot to make sure knot will not slip. Slide napkins through rings for a beautiful finishing touch to your tabletop.

Flamboyant Flowers Wall Art

Sharp angles, soft shapes, interesting textures, and a play of bright fabrics against a more subtle background make this wall piece an eye-catching addition to any room. Rather than a frame, two decorative pieces of molding flank the wall art and feature decorative tacks that accentuate the background angle of the fabric piece.

Materials Needed

Finished size: 24" square

Fabric A (Upper Background) - ⅔ yard
    One 23" x 30" piece
Fabric B (Narrow Stripe) - ⅛ yard
    One 1" x 31" strip
Fabric C (Wide Stripe) - ⅛ yard
    One 1¼" x 31" strip
Fabric D (Lower Background) - ½ yard
    One 15" x 30" piece
Vase Appliqué - ⅓ yard
Flower, Stem and Leaf Appliqués - Assorted scraps
Lightweight Fusible Web - ⅓ yard
Heavyweight Fusible Web - ⅓ yard
Yarns to Match Flower Fabric
Artist Stretcher Bars - Four to make 24" square
Staple Gun & Staples   Decorative Molding - Two 24"-
    long pieces
Delta Ceramcoat Burnt Umber Paint
Sandpaper
Assorted Paintbrushes
Matte Varnish
Burnt Umber Water Based Glaze Effects*
Decorative Tacks
Hot Glue Gun and Glue Sticks
Two Sawtooth Picture Hangers

*This environment friendly glaze is available
at American Unfinished Furniture Stores

Getting Started

Floral appliqués are quick-fused to a pieced 30" background square (unfinished) and embellished with yarn. Heavyweight fusible web is used for the floral appliqués and lightweight fusible for the vase. The project is stapled to artist stretcher bars. For a decorative touch, the wall art is hung between two pieces of wood molding that have been painted and embellished with decorative tacks.

Making the Wall Art

1. Referring to diagram, mark the right side of Fabric A piece (front) 15¼" from top. Mark the left side (front) 22¼" from top. Draw a connecting line between the two marks. Make a diagonal cut following the line.

2. Referring to diagram, mark the right side of Fabric D piece (front) 14" from the bottom. Mark the left side (front) 7" from the bottom. Draw a connecting line between the two marks and cut on drawn line.

3. Following diagram, arrange Fabric A piece, 1" x 31" Fabric B strip, 1¼" x 31" Fabric C strip, and Fabric D piece. Sew together using ¼"-wide seams. Press.

Adding the Appliqués

Refer to appliqué instructions on page 93. Our instructions are for Quick-Fuse Appliqué, but if you prefer hand appliqué, add ¼"-wide seam allowances.

1. Refer to Quick-Fuse Appliqué on page 93, photo, and Wall Art Patterns on page 42 & 43. On paper side of heavyweight fusible web trace two Stems, Flowers 1 and 2, two Flower Centers, four Large Leaves and two reversed, and two Small Leaves and one reversed. On paper side of lightweight fusible web, trace one Vase.

2. Using Vase Fabric and assorted scraps, prepare appliqués for fusing. Refer to photo to position appliqués on Flamboyant Flowers Wall Art background. Prior to fusing place stretcher bars over background to check position of appliqués to frame. Fuse in place. Finish vase edges with satin stitch or other decorative stitching as desired.

3. Referring to photo, glue or couch (page 95) yarn to flowers.

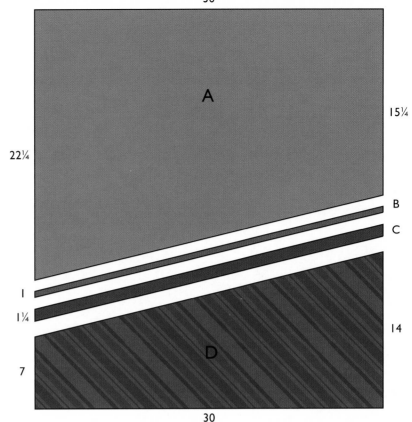

4. Since this piece was designed as wall art, it does not need to be quilted. If quilting is desired, please refer to Layering the Quilt on page 94 and quilt as desired. If quilted, the wall piece can either be finished with binding or mounted on stretcher bars.

5. To mount art piece on stretcher bars, refer to Mounting Fabric Art on page 95 and use 24" stretcher bars.

Preparing the Molding

We used the back side of a common 3"-wide pre-primed molding purchased at a home improvement center for this project. The home improvement center cut the molding to the 24" lengths for us.

1. Refer to General Painting Directions on page 95. Basecoat molding with burnt umber paint and allow to dry. Use sandpaper to distress the edges. Use a damp rag or tack cloth to remove residue.

3. Apply burnt umber glaze. While glaze is wet, pull a dry paintbrush through glaze the entire length of the molding for a wood grain effect.

4. After paint is dry, carefully center and affix hanger to the back side of each molding piece.

5. On a table, place molding on either side of art piece at the distance you want them to hang. Use a ruler and pencil to mark the angles for the decorative tacks. Use a wire cutter to cut the heads off upholstery tacks, then affix to molding with hot glue.

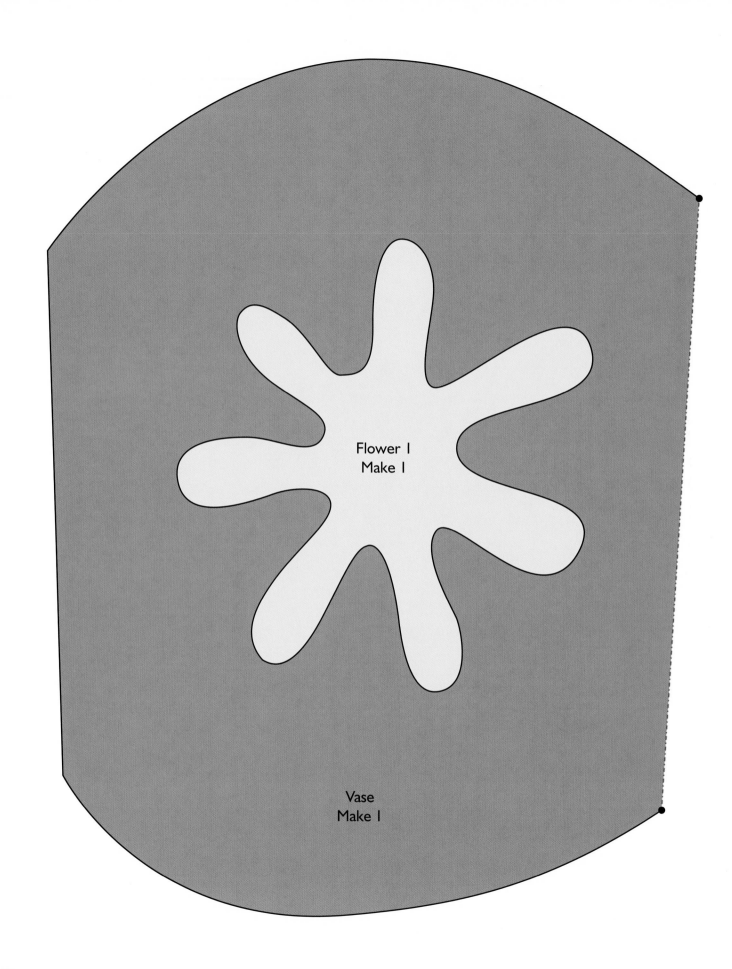

Flower 1
Make 1

Vase
Make 1

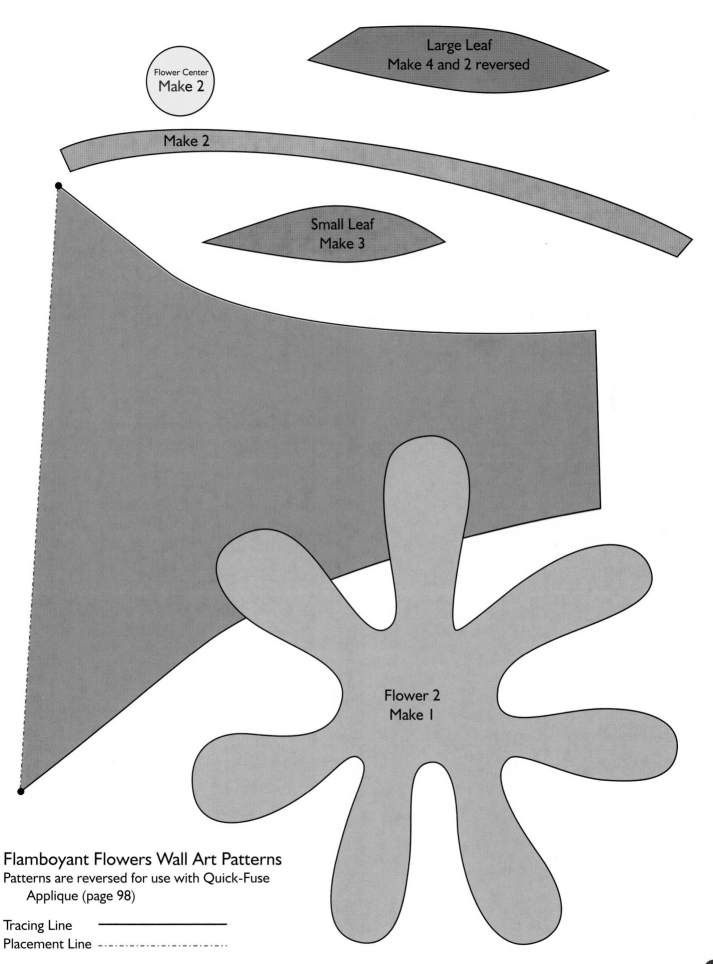

Flower Center
Make 2

Large Leaf
Make 4 and 2 reversed

Make 2

Small Leaf
Make 3

Flower 2
Make 1

Flamboyant Flowers Wall Art Patterns
Patterns are reversed for use with Quick-Fuse
Applique (page 98)

Tracing Line ——————————

Placement Line -·-·-·-·-·-·-·-·-

Rhythm

Repetition of colors,

shapes, and designs

creates a syncopated beat

for the bedroom.

In-tune with modern trends,

the soft furnishings are highlighted

by glossy, dark furniture.

Rhythm & Blues Bed Quilt

Rhythm & Blues Bed Quilt 109" x 100"	FIRST CUT		SECOND CUT	
	Number of Strips or Pieces	Dimensions	Number of Pieces	Dimensions
■ Fabric A Block Centers and Borders 1¼ yards	12	2½" x 42"	12	2½" x 18½"
			12	2½" x 14½"
			12	2½" squares
	8	1½" x 42"	12	1½" x 12½"
			12	1½" x 10½"
■ Fabric B Block 1 Square and Block 2 Triangles ⅞ yard	2	6" x 42"	12	6" squares* *(cut once diagonally)
	4	3½" x 42"	12	3½" x 8½"
			12	3½" x 2½"
▦ Fabric C Block Borders 2 yards	19	3½" x 42"	12	3½" x 18½"
			12	3½" x 14½"
			12	3½" x 12½"
			12	3½" x 8½"
▨ Fabric D Block 2 Square ⅜ yard	4	3" x 42"	12	3" x 7½"
			12	3" x 2½"
■ Piping Fabric ½ yard	5	2¾" x 42"		
BORDERS				
■ Fabric A Brown 2⅓ yards	3	27" x 42"	15	27" x 3½"
			13	27" x 3"
■ Fabric B Blue 2⅓ yards	3	27" x 42"	13	27" x 2½"
			13	27" x 2"
			15	27" x 1½"
▦ Fabric C Tan Geometric 1⅝ yards	2	27" x 42"	2	27" x 3¼"
			13	27" x 3"
			15	27" x 2½"
▨ Fabric D Tan ⅞ yard	1	27" x 42"	2	27" x 2½"
			13	27" x 2"
□ Fabric E Ivory ⅞ yard	1	27" x 42"	26	27" x 1½"
■ Binding 1 yard	11	2¾" x 42"		

Backing - 8⅞ yards
Batting - 117" x 108"
Cord for Piping - 5¾ yards

A rhythmic pattern of colors and squares defines this softly styled bed quilt. Trend-conscious colors team with geometric patterns for a quilt that is at once contemporary and comfortable. Piping and a striped skirt add bedspread-like detail to this easy-to-live-with quilt.

Fabric Requirements and Cutting Instructions

Read all intsructions before beginning and use ¼"-wide seam allowances throughout. Read Cutting Strips and Pieces on page 92 prior to cutting fabrics.

Getting Started

This quilt is designed for a full-size bed and is made of twelve pieced blocks in two designs, each measuring 18½" square (unfinished). The blocks are bordered with wide corded piping. Strip-pieced borders form sides and bottom of the quilt. The strip-pieced borders are 27" long, but may be adjusted to fit the "drop" for your specific bed. We used 27" for a drop of 25", because quilting shortens the border.

Refer to Accurate Seam Allowance on page 92. Whenever possible, use the Assembly Line Method on page 92. Press seams in direction of arrows.

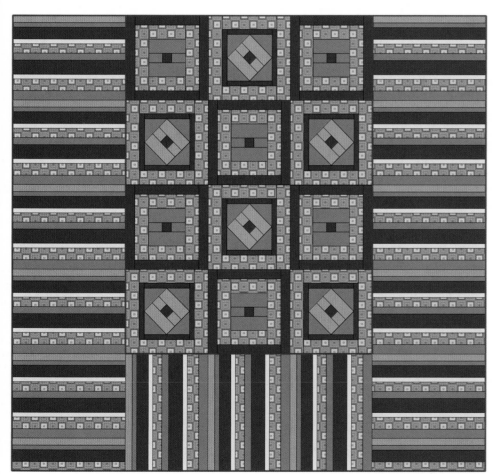

Rhythm & Blues Bed Quilt
Finished Size: 109" x 100"

Making the Blocks

Block One

1. Sew one 2½" Fabric A square between two 3½" x 2½" Fabric B pieces as shown. Press. Make six.

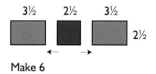

Make 6

2. Arrange and sew two 3½" x 8½" Fabric C pieces, two 3½" x 8½" Fabric B, pieces and unit from step 1 as shown. Press. Make six.

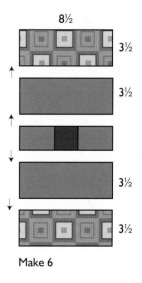

Make 6

3. Sew unit from step 2 between two 3½" x 14½" Fabric C pieces as shown. Press. Make six.

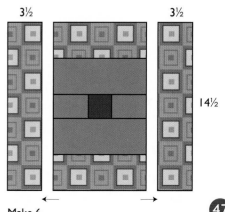

Make 6

4. Sew unit from step 3 between two 2½" x 14½" Fabric A pieces and press toward Fabric A. Sew this unit between two 2½" x 18½" Fabric A pieces as shown. Press. Make six. Block One measures 18½" square.

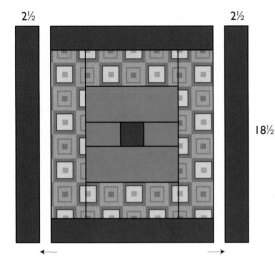

Make 6
Block One measures 18½" square

Block Two

1. Sew one 2½" Fabric A square between two 3" x 2½" Fabric D pieces as shown. Press. Make six.

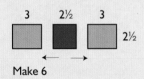

Make 6

2. Sew unit from step 1 between two 3" x 7½" Fabric D pieces as shown. Press. Make six.

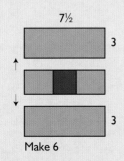

Make 6

3. Sew unit from step 2 between two Fabric B triangles as shown. (Triangle will extend past edge of unit.) Press. Make six.

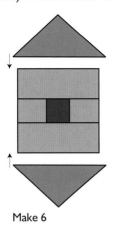

Make 6

4. Sew unit from step 3 between two Fabric B triangles as shown. Press. Square unit to 10½". Make six.

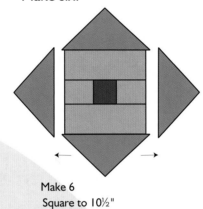

Make 6
Square to 10½"

5. Sew unit from step 4 between two 1½" x 10½" Fabric A pieces as shown. Press. Make six.

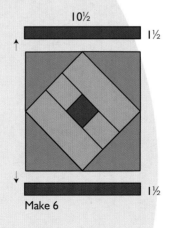

Make 6

6. Sew unit from step 5 between two 1½" x 12½" Fabric A pieces as shown. Press. Make six.

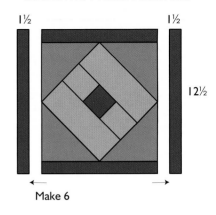

Make 6

7. Sew unit from step 6 between two 3½" x 12½" Fabric C pieces. Press toward Fabric C. Sew this unit between two 3½" x 18½" Fabric C pieces as shown. Press. Make six. Block Two measures 18½" square.

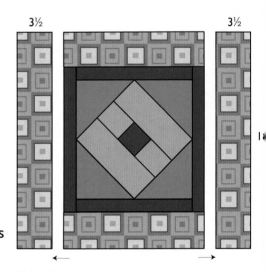

Make 6
Block Two measures 18½" square

8. Referring to photo on page 45 and layout on page 47, arrange and sew Block 1 and Block 2 to make four rows of three blocks each. Press seams in opposite directions from row to row. Sew rows together. Press.

Adding the Piping

1. Sew 2¾" x 42" piping strips together end-to-end to make one 2¾"-wide piping strip. Press.

2. Cover cord with piping strip extending piping one inch beyond edge of cording. Stitch piping cover using ¼"-wide patchwork foot or zipper foot and a basting stitch, stitching close to cording, but leaving a bit of space for the final stitching.

3. Pin piping to right side of quilt top along sides and bottom edge, leaving top edge free of piping. Both ends of piping should extend 1" beyond seam at top of quilt Baste in place.

Making the Borders

1. Arrange and sew together the following pieces as shown: one 27" x 2" Fabric D, one 27" x 1½" Fabric B, one 27" x 3" Fabric A, one 27" x 1½" Fabric E, one 27" x 2½" Fabric C, one 27" x 2" Fabric B, one 27" x 3½" Fabric A, one 27" x 1½" Fabric E, one 27" x 3", Fabric C, and one 27" x 2½" Fabric B. Press. Make thirteen. Unit measures 18½" x 27".

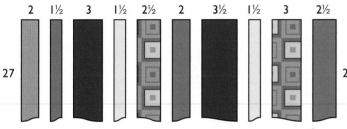

Make 13

2. Sew three units from step 1 together as shown. Press. Referring to photo on page 45 and layout on page 47, pin bottom border unit and quilt top with piping, right sides together, and stitch using a zipper foot. Press seems toward border.

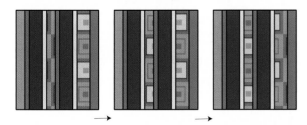

3. Arrange and sew together one 27" x 2½" Fabric D strip, one 27" x 1½" Fabric B strip, one 27" x 3½" Fabric A strip, and one 27" x 3¼" Fabric C strip as shown. Press. Make two.

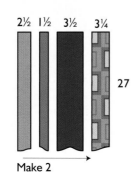

Make 2

4. Referring to layout on page 47, arrange and sew five border units from step 1 and unit from step 3 together to form side borders. Press seams toward step 3 unit. Make two.

5. Referring to photo on page 45 and layout on pages 47, pin units from step 4 to sides of quilt top. Using a zipper foot, stitch quilt top, piping, and side borders together. Press seams toward border.

Layering and Finishing

1. Cut backing fabric crosswise into three equal pieces. Sew pieces together to make one 120" x 100" (approximate) backing piece. Press. Arrange and baste backing, batting and top together, referring to Layering the Quilt on page 94.

2. Hand or machine quilt as desired.

3. Place quilt on bed and adjust length of border to fit "drop" of bed, if needed.

4. To finish edges of piping, baste across edge of piping and trim even with quilt top.

5. Sew 2¾" x 42" binding strips end-to-end to make one 2¾"-wide binding piece. Press. Refer to Binding the Quilt on page 94 and bind quilt to finish, enclosing piping in binding seam.

Upbeat Tempo Wall Art

Finished Size: 26" square

Upbeat Tempo Wall Art 26" Square	FIRST CUT		SECOND CUT	
	Number of Strips or Pieces	Dimensions	Number of Pieces	Dimensions
Fabric A Background & Outside Border ⅞ yard	1 3	8" x 42" 6¼" x 42"	2 2	6¼" x 30" 6¼" x 18½"
Fabric B Tan Background ¼ yard	1	8" x 42"		
Fabric C First Border ⅛ yard	2	1" x 42"	2 2	1" x 13½" 1" x 12½"
Fabric D Second Border ¼ yard	2	3" x 42"	2 2	3" x 18½" 3" x 13½"

Backing - 1 yard
Batting - 34" x 34"
Blue Embroidery Thread or Floss
Stabilizer (For Machine Embroidery)
Artist Stretcher Bars - Four pieces to make 26" square
Staple Gun & Staples
Optional Binding - ⅓ yard
    Three 2¾" x42" Strips

Pick up the design tempo in your bedroom or living room with this in-tune quilted wall piece. Embroidered spirals combine with fabric squares for a contemporary and stylish wall art piece in trend-favored colors. Accent the wall piece and balance your display with easy-to-make display shelves.

Fabric Requirements & Cutting Instructions

Read all instructions before beginning and use ¼"-wide seam allowances throughout. Read Cutting Strips and Pieces on page 92 prior to cutting fabrics.

Getting Started

This wall art consists of a simple nine-patch block embroidered with a spiral design. Three borders complete the top. The quilt is stapled to stretcher bars. For a speedy project, replace the embroidered pieces with bold "fussy cut" fabric squares.

Refer to Accurate Seam Allowance on page 92. Whenever possible, use the Assembly Line Method on page 92. Press seams in direction of arrows.

Embroidering the Background

1. Using a temporary fabric marker, draw 4½" squares on 8" x 42" Fabric A and Fabric B strips spacing squares 2" apart as shown. Draw five squares on Fabric A and four squares on Fabric B.

42

8

2. For machine embroidery, scan and digitize Spiral Pattern on page 52. We used Bernina® artista Software 4.0 and a stem stitch to digitize and embroider nine spirals, one in the center of each marked square.

For hand embroidery, trace Spiral Pattern on page 52 in center of each marked square. Refer to Embroidery Stitch Guide on page 95. Use two strands of embroidery floss and a stem stitch to embroider nine spirals.

3. Using a see-through ruler and rotary cutter, cut five 4½" squares from Fabric A making sure embroidered design is in center of square. Cut four 4½" squares from Fabric B making sure embroidered design is in center of square.

4½

4½

4½

4½

Make 5   Make 4

Making the Top

1. Arrange and sew five 4½" Fabric A squares and four 4½" Fabric B squares in three horizontal rows as shown. Press. Sew rows together and press.

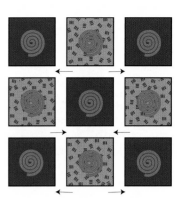

2. Sew unit from step 1 between two 1" x 12½" Fabric C pieces. Press seams toward border. Sew this unit between two 1" x 13½" Fabric C pieces as shown. Press.

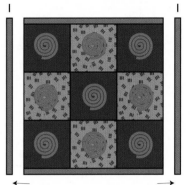

1   1

13½

3. Sew unit from step 2 between two 3" x 13½" Fabric D pieces. Press seams toward border. Sew this unit between two 3" x 18½" Fabric D pieces as shown. Press.

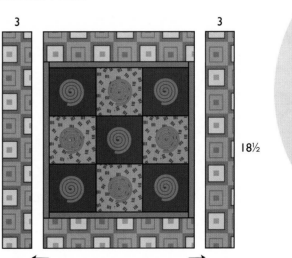

3   3

18½

4. Sew unit from step 3 between two 6¼" x 18½" Fabric A pieces. Press seams toward border. Sew this unit between two 6¼" x 30" Fabric A pieces as shown. Press. Unit measures 30" square.

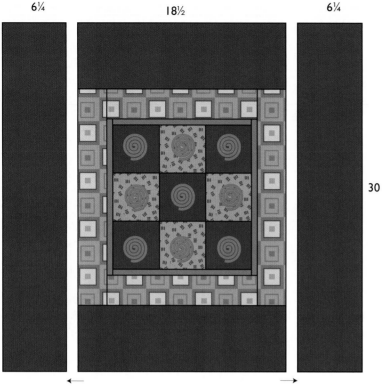

6¼   18½   6¼

30

Unit Measures 30" square

Layering and Finishing

1. Arrange and baste 34" square backing, batting, and top together, referring to Layering the Quilt on page 94. Hand or machine quilt as desired. Trim batting and backing even with top.

2. The quilt can either be stretched on wooden stretcher bars as shown or trimmed to 25½" square and finished with a standard binding.

3. To mount on stretcher bars, refer to Mounting Fabric Art on page 95.

4. To bind, sew three 2¾" x 42" binding strips end-to-end and refer to Binding the Quilt on page 94.

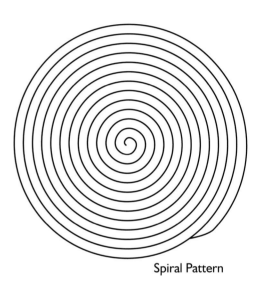

Spiral Pattern

Easy display shelves

Stay on beat with these easy wall shelves to accent a wall art piece or use alone for a designer flourish. We made our shelves from left-over wood pieces from other projects.

Supply List (For two shelves)

1" x 5" Piece of lumber cut into two
    10 ½" lengths (Note: Home improvement stores and lumber yards will often cut the sizes needed when asked).
1" x 3" Piece of Lumber cut into two 7½" lengths
Sandpaper
Wood Glue
Four 1½" Screws
Two Sawtooth Picture Hangers
Delta Ceramcoat® Dark Burnt Umber Paint
Burnt Umber Water Based Glaze Effects *
Matte Varnish

*This environment friendly glaze is available at American Unfinished Furniture Stores. If unavailable, mix a few drops of burnt umber acrylic paint with water-based clear glaze for a substitute.

Displaying Collections

Can't pass an antique shop or yard sale without stepping in? Then you are probably a collector!

From teapots to clocks, garden tools to seashells, most of us find something that warms our hearts and holds our interest enough to amass a collection. Gathered with care and consideration over a period of time, collectibles hold great personal significance for the collector. This emotional meaning makes collectibles a great way to imbue your décor with personality.

Thoughtful placement and arrangement of your collectibles will focus attention on each item, yet allow the assortment to work together as a decorating group. In this bedroom, three wooden wall shelves are grouped together to hold a collection of clocks. The rectangular shelf holds three clocks of similar size and shape. This uniformity allows the eye to focus on each clock individually yet makes the entire shelf work as a unit. Square clocks unite the two square shelves, reinforcing the theme yet making room for other collectibles. By stacking items on top of each other, we create interest while filling the space appropriately.

Don't let your collectibles sit in closets! Look for interesting ways to display your treasures so that you can see them every day.

Making the Shelf

1. Lightly sand wood pieces.

2. Center 7½" piece of wood 3" from bottom of each 10½" wood piece (overlaps approximately 1½" on each side)

3. Drill pilot holes for two screws through both wood pieces for each shelf.

4. Apply wood glue where wood pieces intersect and use screws to hold.

5. Attach sawtooth picture hanger to back of each shelf.

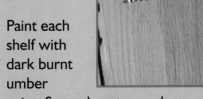

6. Paint each shelf with dark burnt umber paint. Several coats may be required for good coverage.

7. When dry, apply burnt umber glaze to shelves following manufacturer's directions and allow to dry.

8. Apply matte varnish to shelf and allow to dry thoroughly before hanging.

Note: If you plan to set heavy objects on shelves, a sturdier hanging device than the sawtooth picture hanger may be needed. Check your local home improvement store for alternatives.

Tip – Wall shelves and headboard shown in photo on page 45 were painted using these same techniques.

Pillows and more Pillows

Easy pillow shams provide a complementary backdrop for the decorative pillows. Simple geometric quilting and assorted buttons add charm and distinction to these easy pillows.

Buttons Squared Pillow

Finished Size: 13½" square

Materials Needed

Fabric A (Front & Back) - ½ yard
    Two 13½" x 9½" pieces (backing)
    Two 13½" x 6" pieces
    Two 6" x 2½" pieces
Fabric B (Accent) - Scrap
    One 2½" square
Lining - 17½" square
Batting - 17½" square
Eight Assorted Buttons
Pillow Form Fabric - ½ yard
    Two 13½" squares
Polyester Fiberfill

Making the Pillow

1. Sew 2½" Fabric B square between two 6" x 2½" Fabric A pieces as shown. Press.

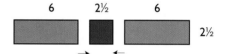

2. Sew unit from step 1 between two 13½" x 6" Fabric A pieces as shown. Press.

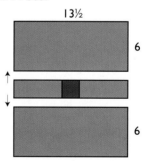

3. Refer to Finishing Pillows, page 95, step 1, to prepare pillow top for quilting. Quilt as desired.

4. Refer to photo. Sew buttons around Accent Square or as desired.

5. Use two 13½" x 9½" Fabric A backing pieces and refer to Finishing Pillows, page 95, steps 2-4 to sew backing and finish pillow.

6. Referring to Pillow Forms, page 95, use two 13½" square pillow form pieces and fiberfill to make pillow form.

Dotted Dashes Pillow

Materials Needed

Fabric A (Front & Back) - ⅝ yard
   One 17½" square
   Two 17½" x 11½" pieces
   (Backing)
Fabric B (Accents Strips) - ⅛ yard
Fabric C (Squares) - Wool Scrap
Lightweight Fusible Web - ⅙ yard
Six ½" Buttons
Lining - 21½" square
Batting - 21½" square
Pillow Form Fabric - ⅝ yard
   Two 17½" squares
Polyester Fiberfill

Making the Pillow

Refer to appliqué instructions on page 93. Our instructions are for Quick-Fuse Appliqué, but if you prefer hand appliqué, add ¼" seam allowances.

1. Refer to Quick-Fuse Appliqué on page 93. On paper side of fusible web, draw two 1" x 13" rectangles and one ½" x 15½" rectangle. Trace six 1¼" squares.

2. Fuse web rectangles to wrong side of Fabric B. Fuse squares to wrong side of Fabric C. Cut rectangles and squares on drawn lines.

Finished size: 17" square

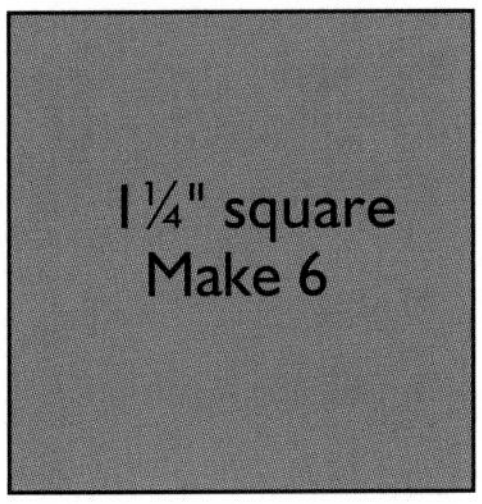

3. Position two 1" x 13" rectangles to right side of 17½" Fabric A square as shown. Trim corners and fuse. Position and fuse six Fabric C squares and ½" x 15½" Fabric B rectangle 1" from and parallel to previously fused strips. Finish appliqué edges with machine satin stitch or other decorative stitching as desired.

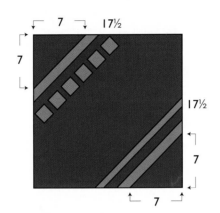

4. Refer to Finishing Pillows, page 95, step 1, to prepare pillow top for quilting. Quilt as desired.

5. Referring to photograph, sew buttons to Fabric B squares on pillow.

6. Refer to Finishing Pillows, page 95, steps 2-4, and use two 17½" x 11½" Fabric A pieces to sew backing.

7. Referring to Pillow Forms, page 95, use two 17½" square pillow form fabric pieces and fiberfill to make 17" square form. Insert pillow form in pillow.

1¼" square
Make 6

Easy Pillow Shams

See photo on page 54
Finished size: 27" x 20"

Materials Needed

Pillow Sham Fabric - 1⅝ yards
   One 27½" x 20½" piece
   Two 27½" x 13½" pieces

Getting Started

This simple project can be made in an hour. It won't take long to transform a plain bed into a comfy, dramatic spot.

Making the Pillow Sham

1. Narrow hem one 27½" edge of one 27½" x 13½" Fabric A piece by folding under ¼" to wrong side. Press. Fold under ¼" again to wrong side and press. Stitch along folded edge. Make two.

2. Overlap pieces from step 1 to make 27½" x 20½" unit. Baste pieces together along edges where they overlap.

3. Place unit from step 2 right sides together with 27½" x 20½" Fabric A piece.

4. Using ¼"-wide seam, sew around all four sides. Trim corners, turn right side out, and press. Insert standard bed pillow.

Imagination

Fresh ideas are born in an environment built to inspire. Your imagination will soar and your productivity will fly in this custom-created craft den. Quotes and photos personalize the desk and a shadow box of collected treasures provides a nest egg of inspiration.

Diamondback Chair

Imagine the difference you can make with a little fabric and thread! An old office chair becomes an inspirational and functional side chair for a cozy craft area when it is creatively upholstered with a quick quilt. To obtain the look of a vintage quilt, this quilt was washed and dried several times before being placed on the chair. Or, use this same technique to make a stunning lap quilt to drape over a chair.

Materials Needed For Chair Cover

Quilt Top Fabric - ⅜ yard each of 18 assorted fabrics
   From each fabric cut three 3½" x 42" strips for a total of fifty-four strips
Backing - 5 yards
Cotton Flannel or Batting - 5 yards or 52" x 90" piece

Getting Started

Use an assortment of light, medium, and dark fabrics to coordinate with room color. We used two dark grays, three medium grays, three medium greens, three light greens, two medium yellows, one lavender, and four light yellows for our chair cover.

Fabrics are sewn into strip-pieced units. Strip-pieced units are sewn together to form a large rectangular quilt. The quilt measures approximately 46" x 84" and should cover the front, back, and sides of a standard office chair. If a larger piece is needed for your chair, make more strip sets and longer rows. The quilt needs to be 10"-12" longer and wider than the chair cushions. After quilting, machine wash and dry the quilt three times to give a soft, aged quality. The quilt will shrink approximately 10%.

Before

Refer to Accurate Seam Allowance on page 92 and use ¼" seams throughout. Whenever possible, use the Assembly Line Method on page 92. Press seams in direction of arrows.

Back and seat cushions of this chair are approximately 20"h x20"w x4"d.

Tip— When sewing several strips together, turn the unit after each addition to alternate the direction of sewing from one row to the next.

Making the Quilt Top

1. Arrange forty-two 3½" x 42" fabric strips in groups of seven. Sew seven strips together as shown. Press. Make six strip sets.

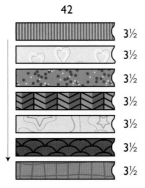

Make 6 in assorted colors

2. Cut each strip set into 3½"-wide segments as shown. Cut sixty-six segments.

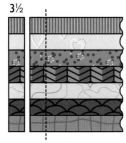

Cut 66 segments

3. Arrange and sew 3½"-wide units from step 2 together to make a row of twenty-one squares, varying arrangement of colors. Press. Make twelve rows.

Make 12

4. Sew six 3½" x 42" fabric strips together as shown to make a strip set. Cut strip set into eleven 3½"-wide segments as shown.

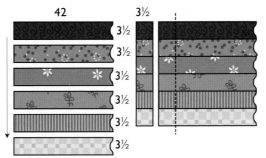

Cut 11 segments

5. Sew three 3½" x 42" fabric strips together to make a strip set. Press. Cut strip set into eleven 3½"-wide segments as shown.

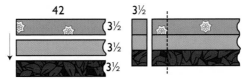

Cut 11 segments

6. Sew two 3½" x 42" fabric strips together as shown to make a strip set. Press. Cut strip set into eleven 3½"-wide segments as shown.

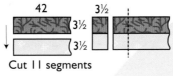

Cut 11 segments

7. Cut remaining 3½" x 42" fabric strip into eleven 3½"-wide squares.

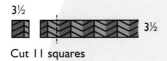

Cut 11 squares

8. Referring to layout on page 61, arrange units from steps 3, 4, 5, 6, and squares from step 7 into rows. Stand back 5 to 10 feet to ensure a pleasing arrangement and concentration of colors. Sew squares and units together to make rows with the following numbers of squares:

Ten rows of 23 squares
Two rows of 21 squares
Two rows of 19 squares
Two rows of 17 squares
Two rows of 15 squares
Two rows of 13 squares
Two rows of 11 squares
Two rows of 9 squares
Two rows of 7 squares
Two rows of 5 squares
Two rows of 3 squares
Two rows of 1 square

9. Sew units and squares together to make rows. Press seams in opposite directions from row to row. There will be some leftover units which may be used to make the Daisy Wall Quilt.

10. Referring to layout on page 61, sew rows together. Press. Using a rotary cutter and see-through ruler, trim triangles from edges along dotted line shown on page 61.

Tip— To make a lap quilt, make only seven rows of twenty-three squares in step 8 for a 46" x 71" (approximate) quilt top. Add borders as desired.

Assembly

1. For 46" x 84" quilt top, cut backing in half crosswise. Sew pieces together to make one 80" x 90" (approximate) backing piece. Press and trim to 52" x 90". If quilt size has been altered, cut backing and batting six inches larger than quilt top.

2. Arrange and baste backing, flannel, and top together referring to Layering the Quilt on page 94. Machine quilt with a large meandering stitch, or as desired. It is NOT recommended to stitch-in-the-ditch.

3. Machine or hand wash the quilt top in warm soapy water and dry in a dryer with a cotton towel. Wash and dry the top three times. This will give an added softness and an aged quality to the quilt top.

Upholstering the Chair

Supply List

> Delta Ceramcoat® Acrylic
>   Craft Paint - Charcoal
> Sandpaper
> Paintbrushes
> Staple Gun and Staples
> Spray Matte Varnish
> Office Chair

Because an office chair has straight lines and simple cushions, the chair is fairly easy to upholster, even for beginners. To finish the wood frame, a 'wash' of charcoal paint was used so that the wood grain shows through the color.

1. Unscrew chair seat and back and remove from wooden frame.

2. Sand frame to remove gloss and wipe off sanding residue. Mix Charcoal paint with water to create a 'wash' and apply to chair frame with paintbrush. Wipe off or add more as needed to achieve color desired. When thoroughly dry, spray chair frame with matte varnish to protect the finish.

3. If chair has separate seat and back, lay the seat on the quilt, making sure there is plenty of quilt to wrap around the sides to allow for stapling on underside of seat. Use a removable marker to mark a cutting line on the quilt for the seat bottom. Wrap the quilt up and over the seat back, allowing room to staple back where staples won't be seen. If there is plenty of fabric, cut on marked line. If not, try changing the positions of the seat and back to make better use of quilted piece.

4. If seat and back are attached, stretch quilted piece over seat, allowing plenty in front to tuck under and staple. Tuck quilted piece into area between seat and back, then stretch quilted piece up and over back, making sure that you have plenty to tuck under the bottom and staple.

5. Staple quilted piece to seat bottom, starting in the middle on front and sides, pulling taut, and stapling at 2" intervals.

6. Keeping quilted piece tightly tucked between seat and back, fold quilted piece over top of chair back. Wrap quilted piece around sides of the back, trim excess fabric if needed, then pull fabric snugly over the back as shown. Staple in place.

7. Fold side fabric and pull taut at angle where back and seat connect. Clip if needed. Work until smooth and staple in place.

8. Put cushions back on chair frame and use screws to hold in place.

Diamondback Chair Cover
Approximate Size: 46" x 85"

Imagination Desk

Imagine a spot of your own where creativity is encouraged and finished projects are celebrated. Create your own inspirational refuge with a thrift store desk, photos, and bits and pieces of left-over trims and scrapbook supplies.

Supply List

Wooden Desk
¼" Thick MDF Board Cut to Fit
    Desktop
Sandpaper
Assorted Paintbrushes
Decoupage Glue
Assorted Photos, Ribbon, & Trims
Scrapbook Supplies - Card stock,
    quotes on vellum, stick-on letters
    & brown shading chalk (for adding
    shadows to paper & photo edges)
Delta Ceramcoat® Acrylic Paint -
    Medium Victorian Teal
Burnt Umber Water Based Glaze
    Effects*

*This environment friendly glaze is available at American Unfinished Furniture Stores. If unavailable, mix a few drops of burnt umber acrylic paint with water-based clear glaze for a substitute.

Painting the Desk

1. Refer to General Painting Directions on page 95. Since decoupage is hard to remove, a piece of MDF board was cut to the size of desktop for this project. This way, the decoupaged design can be removed if desired sometime in the future, just by removing the MDF board.

2. Fill any cracks or mars with wood filler. Sand desk thoroughly to remove shine and any peeling paint. Sand MDF board lightly. Use a tack cloth or damp rag to remove residue.

3. Paint desk with Medium Victorian Teal paint. Two or more coats may be required for good coverage. Allow to dry completely between coats. We chose to leave the MDF board its natural color, but if desired, paint board the same or a complementary color.

4. Sand edges of desk to distress. Apply Burnt Umber Glaze to age desk.

Decoupage Decor

Select photos from favorite past projects that you want to display. We chose to print the photos on a computer printer using sepia tones. Using patterns on page 65, cut daisies from card stock, shadowing edges with brown chalk. Decide on placement of photos, inspirational sayings, words, trims, and daisies. Using decoupage, apply ribbon, daisies, trims and rickrack first following directions on decoupage jar. Allow to dry, then apply several coats of decoupage over trims. When completely dry, use decoupage to adhere other decorations onto board, overlapping items as desired. When dry, coat entire surface with several coats of decoupage.

bits n pieces boxes

Corral your trims and buttons and beads in cute storage boxes. You'll be inspired every time you pull out one of these too-cute creations.

Supply List:

Two Cardboard Photo Storage Boxes
Americana® Acrylic Craft Paint - Buttermilk
Paintbrush
Assorted Trims, Beads, and Buttons
Yellow Card Stock
Brown Shading Chalk
Letter Stickers
Mod Podge® Matte (decoupage glue)

1. Remove box lids from bases and paint each piece with Buttermilk paint. Two coats may be required for good coverage. Allow to dry thoroughly after each coat of paint.

2. Using Large Daisy pattern on page 65, cut two daisies from card stock and darken edges with brown chalk as shown at right.

3. Referring to photo, draw a soft pencil line as a guideline for words. Use letter stickers to spell out "BEADS" and "BUTTONS" on one box, and "TRIMS" on the other box. Glue daisies in place on each box with decoupage.

4. Referring to photo, use decoupage to adhere trims to each box as shown in photo. When trims are completely dry, coat each lid with several coats of decoupage.

5. Glue beads and buttons to box and make a label for end of each box.

Treasure Box

Display small treasures that are dear to your heart and that spark your imagination in this unique shadow box. We made our own display box, but you can also find similar items at craft and discount stores. We added a touch of art deco trim to our shadow box, repeating an element found in the desk.

Supply List

Poplar Boards:
  Outside Frame: 2½" wide by ½"-thick - Approximately 7½ running feet
  Inside Dividers: 2¼" wide by ¼"-thick - Approximately 9 running feet.
MDF Board for Backing: 17½" x 23½", ¼" - thick.
Wood Glue
Small Nails
Sandpaper
Delta Ceramcoat® Acrylic Paints - Medium Victorian Teal and Charcoal
Assorted Paintbrushes

Making the Shadow Box

This project requires a skilled craftsman who is accustomed to working with power tools. Follow all safety precautions suggested by tool manufacturers.

1. Mitering corners, cut Outside Frame boards to make an 18" x 24" (outside measurement) frame. Do not glue. On each of the long boards, mark points at 5¾", 11½", and 17¼" as shown. On each of short boards, mark points at 5 ⅝ " and 11 ⁵⁄₁₆" as shown.

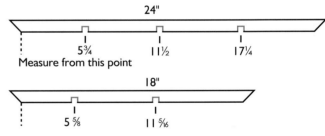

2. Using marks as center points, use a table saw to cut a ¼" square groove, the entire width of the board, at each marked point. Make sure each groove is the correct size to fit one of the Inside Divider boards.

3. Glue and nail Outside Frame, making sure all corners are right angles. Allow glue to dry overnight.

4. Cut Inside Divider boards to length to fit in grooves in frame. (Two boards approximately 23⅜ " and three boards approximately 17⅜ ").

5. Using a table saw, cut grooves about half way through each Inside Divider board so boards fit together. Install Inside Dividers and glue at ends to hold in place.

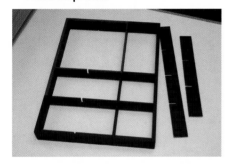

6. Cut a groove into the back of frame and inset backing board.

7. If Art Deco trim is desired, transfer pattern onto a piece of left-over Inside Divider board. Cut out two trim pieces. Trim will be installed after painting.

Painting the Shadow Box

1. Sand all joints and any rough spots on boards. Remove sanding residue with tack cloth or damp rag. Paint shadow box with Charcoal paint. Two coats may be required for good coverage. Allow to dry completely between coats of paint.

2. When thoroughly dry, sand edges of shadow box for a distressed look.

3. Paint Art Deco trim with Medium Victorian Teal paint and allow to dry. Sand edges. Mix a couple drops of Charcoal paint with water. Brush onto trim pieces, wiping paint away or adding more as desired for a distressed look. When dry, glue trim pieces to shadow box as shown in photo.

Decorating the Shadow Box

Select a variety of small special treasures to showcase in your shadow box. Photos in frames, natural elements like rocks and shells, old wooden spools with bright colored threads, glass bottles, and small ceramic figurines are among the items we chose. Fabric items like the pillow and lilac sachet add softness. Some left-over mosaic tiles serve as a background element in two of the cubby holes while a large "C" personalizes the display.

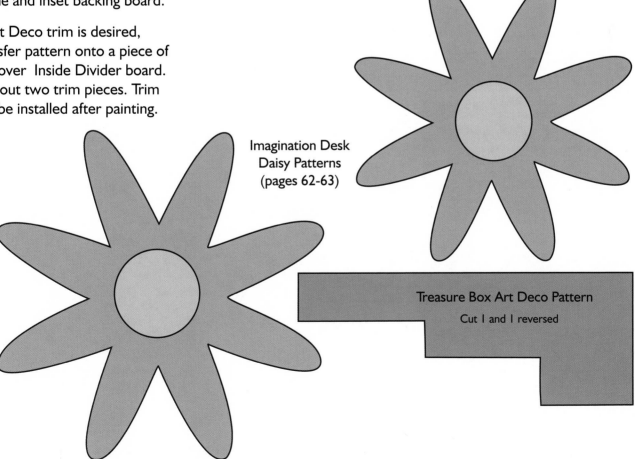

Imagination Desk
Daisy Patterns
(pages 62-63)

Treasure Box Art Deco Pattern
Cut 1 and 1 reversed

Daisy Wall Quilt

This cheery and good-natured wall quilt makes a sweet and simple decor statement. Or, use this idea to make a lap quilt, alternating daisy and patchwork blocks. The pattern can also be adapted to make a pillow such as the one shown on page 58.

Materials Needed

Daisy Background - ½ yard
  15½" Square
Border - Assorted Scraps
  Fifty-Six 3½" square pieces (we used 15 fabrics)
Daisy Appliqué - ⅜ yard
Binding - ⅜ yard
  Four 2¾" x 42" strips
Backing - 1 yard
Batting - 32" square piece
Lightweight Fusible Web - ⅜ yard
Assorted Decorative Beads
Unique Stitch® Fabric Glue

Getting Started

Pieced squares border an appliquéd center square for a bright and cheerful wallhanging. Decorative beads form the center of the daisy and are glued on for easy application. Leftover strip-pieced units from Diamondback Chair Cover can be used to make this wall quilt.

Adding the Appliqué

Refer to appliqué instructions on page 93. Our instructions are for Quick-Fuse Appliqué, but if you prefer hand appliqué, add ¼" seam allowances.

1. Refer to Quick-Fuse Appliqué on page 93, photo, and Daisy Wall Quilt Pattern. On paper side of fusible web, trace Daisy Wall Quilt Pattern.

2. Use Daisy Appliqué Fabric to prepare appliqué for fusing.

3. Referring to photo, position and fuse daisy to 15½" Fabric A square. Finish edges with satin stitch or other decorative machine stitching as desired.

Making the Pieced Border

1. Sew five assorted 3½" Fabric B squares together as shown. Press. Make eight units.

Make 8

2. Sew two units from step 1 together as shown. Press. Make four.

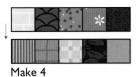

Make 4

3. Sew appliquéd Fabric A square between two units from step 2 as shown. Press.

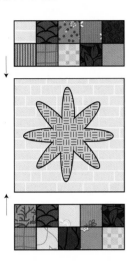

4. Sew two 3½" Fabric B squares together as shown. Press. Make eight assorted units.

3½   3½   3½

Make 8 in assorted colors

5. Arrange and sew four units from step 4 and one unit from step 2 together as shown. Press. Make two.

6. Referring to photo and layout, sew unit from step 3 between units from step 5.

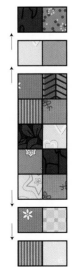

Make 2

Daisy Wall Quilt Pattern
¼ Wallhanging Applique

Trace 4 times aligning placement lines to make one daisy

Layering and Finishing

1. Cut backing fabric to 32" x 32". Arrange and baste backing, batting, and top together referring to Layering the Quilt on page 94. Hand or machine quilt as desired.

2. Refer to Binding the Quilt on page 94 and bind quilt to finish.

3. Referring to photo, glue or sew decorative beads to center of daisy appliqué.

Dasiy Wall Quilt
Finished Size: 28" Square

Sophistication

Mix an assortment of fabrications

with artful assurance

to create a sophisticated grouping

of fabric wall art and

soft furnishings for the living room.

Sheen, touch, and texture

are important design elements

for this tasteful, chic look.

Elegance Squared Throw

Elegance Squared Throw 43" x 57"	FIRST CUT		SECOND CUT	
	Number of Strips or Pieces	Dimensions	Number of Pieces	Dimensions
■ Fabric A Block Centers ¼ yard	2 1	2½" x 42" 1½" x 42"		
■ Fabric B Narrow Block Borders 1 yard	2 2 9*	5½" x 42" 3½" x 42" 1½" x 42"	34 36 34	5½" x 1½" 3½" x 1½" 1½" x 7½"
	*Two will be used for strip set			
▦ Fabric C Wide Block Borders 1⅝ yards	3 2 4 4	7½" x 42" 5½" x 42" 2½" x 42" 2" x 42"	36 34 36	7½" x 2½" 5½" x 2" 2½" x 3½"
BORDERS				
■ First Border ¼ yard	5	1¼" x 42"		
▦ Outside Border 1⅜ yards OR ⅝ yard	1 3 5	37" x 42" 3¼" x 42" 3¼" x 42"	2	37" x 3¼" (Excess may be used for binding)
▦ Binding ⅝ yard	6	2¾" x 42"		

Backing - 2¾ yards
Batting - 49" x 63"

Many decorator fabrics have nap. The fabrics on the chart are cut to ensure that all of Fabric B is going in the same direction in the blocks. All of Fabric C is going in the same direction, but grain is opposite of Fabric B.

Decorator fabrics in a variety of textures and sheens make this graphically-appealing throw an elegant addition to any room. The play of fabric sheens makes this quilt look sophisticated, yet is remarkably easy to construct.

Fabric Requirements & Cutting Instructions

Read all instructions before beginning and use ¼"-wide seam allowances throughout. Read Cutting Strips and Pieces on page 92 prior to cutting fabrics.

Getting Started

This quilt consists of two styles of blocks 7½" square (unfinished). Simple piecing and strip-piecing make this an easy project. If using decorator fabric, determine if the fabric is directional or has nap. The cutting chart allows for nap, but make sure it will work with your fabric.

Refer to Accurate Seam Allowance on page 92. Whenever possible, use the Assembly Line Method on page 92. Press seams in direction of arrows.

Making Block One

1. Sew 1½" x 42" Fabric A strip between two 1½" x 42" Fabric B strips as shown. Press. Cut strip set into eighteen 1½"-wide segments.

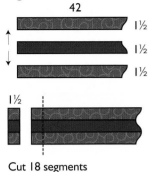

42

1½

1½

1½

1½

Cut 18 segments

2. Sew one unit from step 1 between two 3½" x 1½" Fabric B pieces. Press. Make eighteen.

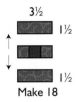

3½

1½

1½

Make 18

3. Sew one unit from step 2 between two 2½" x 3 ½" Fabric C pieces as shown. Press. Make eighteen.

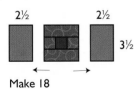

2½   2½

3½

Make 18

4. Sew one unit from step 3 between two 7½" x 2½" Fabric C pieces as shown. Press. Make eighteen. Block One measures 7½" square.

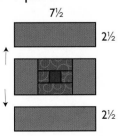

7½

2½

2½

Make 18
Block One measures 7½" square

Making Block Two

1. Sew one 2½" x 42" Fabric A strip between two 2" x 42" Fabric C strips as shown. Press. Make two. Cut strip sets into seventeen 2½"-wide segments.

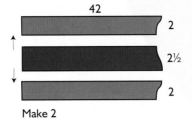

42

2

2½

2

Make 2

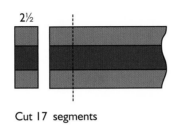

2½

Cut 17 segments

2. Arrange and sew two 5½" x 1½" Fabric B pieces, two 5½" x 2" Fabric C pieces, and one unit from step 1 together as shown. Press. Make seventeen.

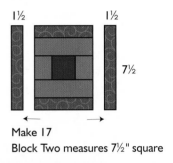

5½

1½

2

2

1½

Make 17

3. Sew unit from step 2 between two 1½" x 7½" Fabric B pieces as shown. Press. Make seventeen. Block Two measures 7½" square.

1½   1½

7½

Make 17
Block Two measures 7½" square

Elegance Squared Throw
Finished Size: 43" x 57"

Assembly

1. Arrange and sew three of Block One and two of Block Two as shown to make a row. Press. Make four.

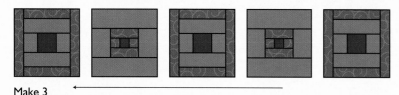

Make 4 →

2. Arrange and sew three of Block Two and two of Block One as shown to make a row. Press. Make three.

Make 3 ←

3. Referring to photo on page 70 and layout on page 71, sew rows together. Press.

multi metal lamp

A plain brass lamp found at a yard sale becomes a unique decorating accessory when silver leaf is added to the base and ribbon and tack trim to the shade. Silver leafing is messy, but easy to do, and can change just about anything into a beautiful silvery accessory.

Supply List

Floor Lamp & Shade
Mona Lisa Silver Leaf & Metal Leaf
   Adhesive Size
Assorted Paintbrushes
McCloskey® Special Effects™
   Aging Glaze
Ribbon - ½"-wide Brown &
   ⅛"-wide Green
Elmer's® Craft Bond Extra-
   Strength Spray Adhesive
Tacky Glue
Decorative Tacks

1. Read and follow all instructions on products. Select areas to be silver leafed on lamp. Apply a thin coat of Metal Leaf Adhesive to areas selected and allow to set until tacky (about 30 minutes).

Adding the Borders

1. Refer to Adding the Borders on page 94. Measure quilt through center from side to side. Cut two 1¼"-wide First Border strips to that measurement. Sew to top and bottom of quilt. Press seams toward border.

2. Sew remaining 1¼" x 42" First Border strips end-to-end to make one 1¼"-wide border strip. Press. Measure quilt through center from top to bottom including borders just added. Cut two 1¼"-wide First Border strips to that measurement. Sew to sides of quilt. Press.

3. Sew 37" x 3¼" Outside Border strips to top and bottom of quilt. Press seams toward border.

4. Sew 3¼" x 42" Outside Border strips end-to-end to make one 3¼"-wide border strip. Press. Measure quilt through center from top to bottom including borders just added. Cut two 3¼"-wide Outside Border strips to that measurement. Sew to sides of quilt. Press.

Layering and Finishing

1. Cut backing in half crosswise. Sew pieces together to make one 49" x 80" (approximate) backing piece. Press and trim to 49" x 63".

2. Arrange and baste backing, batting, and top together referring to Layering the Quilt on page 94. Hand or machine quilt as desired.

3. Sew 2¾" binding strips end-to-end to make one continuous 2¾"-wide binding strip. Refer to Binding the Quilt on page 94 and bind quilt to finish.

---

2. Place sheet of silver leaf over adhesive area and using a soft paintbrush adhere leaf to adhesive. Repeat this process until all the selected areas are covered with silver leaf. Use dry paintbrush to brush away excess silver leaf.

Apply Silver Leaf

3. Using a paintbrush, apply Aging Glaze to silver leaf areas. The Aging Glaze will help blend silver and brass areas.

Apply Aging Glaze

4. To decorate the shade, apply ribbons to edge of shade following instructions for Color-Banded Chandelier on page 38. Using a wire cutter, cut heads from upholstery tacks and adhere to shade using a tacky glue.

Quilted Wall Art

Fabric pieces become fine art when a mix of fabrics and textures are used in the construction, and small quilts receive a sophisticated finish by using artist stretcher bars. This grouping features a variety of sizes, fabrications, and techniques that work together because of a cohesive color scheme.

Square on Square Wall Art

The beautiful sofa throw design becomes wall art when the pattern is adapted to allow for stretcher bars. Attractive in this distinctive grouping, this wall piece would add a sophisticated touch to any room.

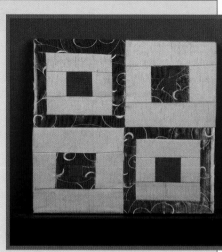

Finished Size: 14" square

Square on Square Wall Art 14" x 14"	FIRST CUT		SECOND CUT	
	Number of Strips or Pieces	Dimensions	Number of Pieces	Dimensions
Fabric A Block Centers Scrap	2 2	2½" squares 1½" squares		
Fabric B Narrow Block Borders ⅜ yard	1	10½" x 42"	2 2 2 4 2 4	10½" x 4½"* 10½" x 1½"* 4½" x 5½" 3½" x 1½" 1½" x 5½" 1½" squares
Fabric C Wide Block Borders ⅜ yard	1	10½" x 42"	2 2 2 4 2 4	10½" x 5½"*" 10½" x 2½"*" 5½" x 3½" 5½" x 2" 3½" x 2½" 2½" x 2"

Staple Gun and Staples
Artist Stretcher Bars - Four to make 14" square

*For directional fabric, the size that is listed first runs parallel to selvage.

Fabric Requirements & Cutting Instructions

Read all instructions before beginning and use ¼"-wide seam allowances throughout. Read Cutting Strips and Pieces on page 92 prior to cutting fabrics.

Getting Started

The Elegance Squared Throw design is adapted for this project to accommodate the use of artist stretcher bars as a finishing technique. Instead of square blocks, the design consists of four off-center blocks that measure

10½" square unfinished. The quilt is stapled to artist stretcher bars so fabric needed to attach the quilt is part of the block.

Refer to Accurate Seam Allowance on page 92. Whenever possible, use the Assembly Line Method on page 92. Press seams in direction of arrows.

Making Block One

1. Sew one 2½" Fabric A square between two 2½" x 2" Fabric C pieces as shown. Press. Make two.

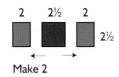

Make 2

2. Sew unit from step 1 between two 5½" x 2" Fabric C pieces as shown. Press. Make two.

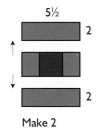

Make 2

3. Sew unit from step 2 between one 4½" x 5½" Fabric B piece and one 1½" x 5½" Fabric B piece as shown. Press. Make two.

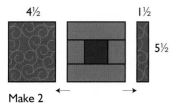

Make 2

4. Sew unit from step 3 between one 10½" x 4½" Fabric B piece and one 10½" x"1½ Fabric B piece as shown. Press. Make two. Block One measures 10½" square.

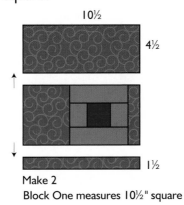

Make 2
Block One measures 10½" square

Making Block Two

1. Sew one 1½" Fabric A square between two 1½" Fabric B squares as shown. Press. Make two.

Make 2

2. Sew unit from step 1 between two 3½" x 1½" Fabric B pieces as shown. Press. Make two.

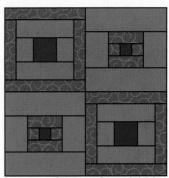

Make 2

3. Sew unit from step 2 between one 3½" x 2½" Fabric C piece and one 5½" x 3½" Fabric C piece as shown. Press. Make two.

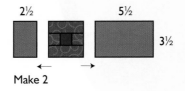

Make 2

4. Sew unit from step 3 between one 10½" x 5½" Fabric C piece and one 10½" x 2½" Fabric C piece as shown. Press. Make two. Block Two measures 10½" square.

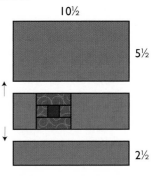

Make 2
Block Two measures 10½" square

Assembly

1. Refering to photo and layout, sew Block One and Block Two together to make a row. Press. Make two.

2. Sew rows together. Press.

3. Refer to Mounting Fabric Art on page 95 and use 14" stretcher bars to attach quilt to stretcher bars.

Square on Square Wall Art
Finished size: 14" square

Curlicue Wall Art

Swirls and Curls in wool and metal flow through this unique wall piece which can easily be made in a few hours. Hand-couched yarn defines the flowing design while curlicue buttons add a metallic gleam.

Quick-fuse applique makes short work of adding the swirls and blossoms.

Finished size: 18" square

Materials Needed

Fabric A (Background) - ¾ yard wool
   One 26" square
Fabric B (Swirls & Curls) - ⅛ yard wool
Fabric C (Blossom Appliqués) - ⅛ yard cotton
Fabric D (Blossom Accent Appliqués) - ⅛ yard wool
Heavyweight Fusible Web - ¼ yard
Lightweight Fusible Web - ¼ yard
Dark Brown Cord or Yarn - ¾ yard
Fourteen Curlicue Buttons
Artist Stretcher Bars - Four pieces to make 18" square

Getting Started

Wool and cotton appliqués fused to a wool background add a visual dimension to this wall art. The project is embellished with wool yarn and buttons that imitate the appliqué. Lightweight fusible web is used for cotton appliqués and heavyweight for wool appliqués.

Making the Background

Refer to appliqué instructions on page 93. Our instructions are for Quick-Fuse Appliqué, but if you prefer hand appliqué, add ¼" seam allowances. We recommend using stabilizer for machine appliqué.

1. Refer to Quick-Fuse Appliqué on page 93 and appliqué patterns below. On paper side of fusible web, trace six Blossoms, six Blossom Accents, four Large Swirls, and six Small Curls.

2. Using Fabrics B, C, and D, prepare appliqués for fusing. Refer to photo to position appliqués on 26" Fabric A square. Prior to fusing, place stretcher bars over background to check appliqué position to frame. Fuse appliqués in place.

3. Finish appliqué edges with machine satin stitch or other decorative stitching as desired. To keep this project quick and easy, we chose to use a satin stitch to finish only the cotton edges.

4. Referring to Couching Technique on page 95 and photo, arrange cord or yarn on background and couch by hand or machine. Referring to photo, position and stitch buttons in place.

5. Refer to Mounting Fabric Art on page 95 and use 18" stretcher bars to attach wall art to frame.

Blossom
Make 6

Large Swirl
Make 2 as shown
Make 2 reversed

Horizon Wall Art

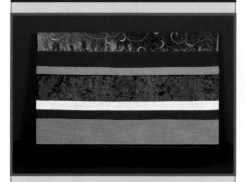

Finished size : 20" x 12"

Beautiful fabrics and rich colors are all it takes to make a distinctive wall piece. A combination of silk blends, cottons, and velour are arranged in carefully considered horizontal bands for this fabric wall piece.

Materials Needed

Fabric A (Embroidered Strip) - ⅙ yard
   One 5¼" x 26" strip
Fabric B (Garnet Strip) - ⅙ yard
   One 2¼" x 26" strip
   One 1½" x 26" strip
Fabric C (Green Strip) - ⅛ yard
   One 1¼" x 26" strip
Fabric D (Velour Strip) - ⅛ yard
   One 3¼" x 26" strip
Fabric E (Ivory Strip) - ⅛ yard
   One 1½" x 26" strip
Fabric F (Nubby Silk Strip) - ¼ yard
   One 6¼" x 26" strip
Fusible Interfacing (Optional) - ¾ yard
Artist Stretcher Bars - Two 20" and
   Two 12"

Getting Started

Tip - When using slinky type fabrics, such as a lightweight velour, press fusible interfacing to wrong side of fabric, prior to cutting, to provide stability when cutting and sewing.

Home decorator and cotton quilting fabrics are strip-pieced for a textural and visual piece of wall art that is fast and simple to make.

Refer to Accurate Seam Allowance on page 92. Use ¼"-wide seams. Press in one direction.

Making the Wall Art

1. Arrange and sew together all fabric strips in the following order:

    5¼" x 26" Fabric A
    2¼" x 26" Fabric B
    1¼" x 26" Fabric C
    3¼" x 26" Fabric D
    1½" x 26" Fabric E
    1½" x 26" Fabric B
    6¼" x 26" Fabric F

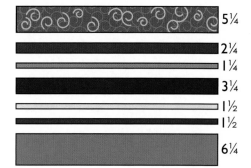

2. Refer to Mounting Fabric Art on page 95 and use 20" and 12" stretcher bars to form a rectangle. Referring to photo, attach fabric unit to stretcher frame, being careful to keep lines straight and parallel to bottom edge.

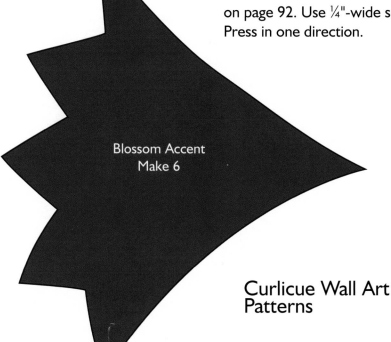

Blossom Accent
Make 6

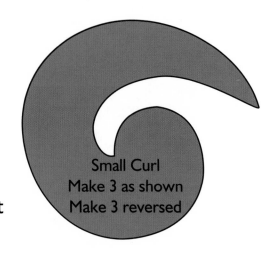

Small Curl
Make 3 as shown
Make 3 reversed

Curlicue Wall Art Patterns

Expression

Express your eclectic self with a mix of contemporary and classic. An easygoing, yet artsy look will bring a touch of mystery to your style. The easy-to-live-with, yet fashion-forward palette, lends itself to a modern wallhanging, box pillows and a classic quilt.